Archival Theory, Records, and the Public

Trevor Livelton

The Society of American Archivists
and
The Scarecrow Press, Inc.
Lanham, Md., & London
1996

This book is based on the author's master's thesis, "Public Records: A Study in Archival Theory," University of British Columbia, 1991.

SCARECROW PRESS, INC.

Published in the United States of America
by The Society of American Archivists and Scarecrow Press, Inc.
4720 Boston Way
Lanham, Maryland 20706

4 Pleydell Gardens, Folkestone
Kent CT20 2DN, England

British Cataloguing-in-Publication Information Available

Library of Congress Cataloging-in-Publication Data

Livelton, Trevor.
        Archival theory, records, and the public / Trevor Livelton.
            p.   cm.
        Originally presented as the author's thesis (master's—British Columbia)
        Includes bibliographical references and index.
        ISBN 0-8108-3051-5 (cloth : alk. paper)
        1. Archives.   2. Public records.   I. Title.
    CD947.L58   1996
    027—dc20   95-26792

ISBN 0-8108- 3051-5 (cloth: alk. paper)

        The paper used in this publication meets the minimum requirements of
American National Standard for Information Sciences—Permanence of Paper for
Printed Library Materials, ANSI Z39.48-1984.
Manufactured in the United States of America.

Contents

Acknowledgments

Among the many persons to whom I am indebted for seeing this work through to its present stage, two deserve special mention. Over the years, both Terry Eastwood and Luciana Duranti have given unstintingly of their time and talents, offering a very special combination of encouragement and thoughtful criticism from first to last. One could not ask for better teachers or more steadfast friends. To them, as to all who contributed in various ways, my heartfelt thanks.

Introduction

This study examines the nature of public records from an archival perspective. It does so in a general or theoretical way, providing an analysis of concepts rather than a practical guide through the daily realities with which public records archivists must deal. While a need for such practical guidance certainly exists, there are others more qualified to take on that important job. This work attempts the more limited task of plowing some basic conceptual ground. It would naturally be gratifying if others were to find this spadework useful for practical ends. However, while convinced that the quality of archival practice rests to a large extent, at least in the long run, on the quality of the theory that underlies it, my primary aim here has been to gain a clearer view of the concepts involved in understanding the nature of public records.

The reason for this overall approach lies partly in the genesis of this study, which began as a thesis in the Master of Archival Studies Program at the University of British Columbia. In an academic environment, one naturally spends a good deal of time attempting to puzzle out the basics by examining definitions found in the professional literature. Close study of these texts almost inevitably reveals a lack of consistency and coherence between various definitions set down by different authors at different times for different purposes, inviting the conclusion that a number of basic questions merit continuing examination. This conclusion may become blunted to some degree by the press of everyday work as one moves from the academy to the workplace, but it does not change. If anything, the fundamental questions gain in vital interest as one comes to realize that tacit answers to them color the fabric of daily work.

How best, for example, to characterize the relation between the concepts of archives and records? Schellenberg's influential discussion of this issue has not found universal acceptance, and there has even been some suggestion that his distinction between the two has become obsolete.[1] Nor is there overall agreement on the nature of the public as a records-creating entity—or even if that is the only or best way to depict the nature of the *public* in public records. Are public records only those of the government? Where can a principled line between public and nonpublic records be drawn? Are the concepts we often take for granted in this regard unique to our own circumstances, or can they be applied universally? The means of exploring such questions also pose some difficulty, since archivists have not been in total agreement about the nature of the theory underlying their work. How best, then, to characterize archival theory, particularly as a means of conceptual exploration? From my perspective as a student and a public records archivist, a theoretical study of the nature of public records has seemed the most straightforward way of approaching such questions.

This context should explain several peculiarities of the present study. For one thing, this is indeed "a tedious and meticulous book," to borrow the words of Muller, Feith, and Fruin.[2] I mention such distinguished forebears, however, not just to warn the reader of certain technical details which, if somewhat inelegant, have nonetheless seemed to require spelling out for the sake of the argument. I also mention them to acknowledge that this book rests on the shoulders of giants, especially Jenkinson and Schellenberg, and may reasonably be viewed as an essentially conservative venture. When one begins with a measure of puzzlement, it can often prove useful to return initially to ideas and methods that have proven their value over time. The discussion of archives and records in chapter 3, for example, attempts to build on a long-held definition of archives, pressing the rest against it. The subsequent discussion of public records, likewise conservative, takes the old notion of the reciprocal relationship between authority and obedience—rulers and ruled, sovereign and subjects—and applies it to one area of the archival world. It is a view that has existed implicitly among archivists for some time in the notion of the accountability of records creators in a democratic society, one I believe may hold a key to a fuller understanding of the meaning and purpose of archival work. The present study, however, does little more than draw attention to the conceptual underpinnings of that notion. The concept of theory offered here is also remarkably conservative. It is essentially nothing more than the age-old concept of philosophical or conceptual analysis (or one version of it) as it can be applied to archival questions. As readers will readily note, this method does little more than extend the approach with which Jenkinson, Schellenberg, and the Dutch (among others) saw fit to begin their respective examinations of the archival world—by defining terms and clarifying concepts.[3]

That the archival world has expanded since these pioneers wrote is beyond doubt. Implicit in the present work, for example, is the assumption that a single volume can no longer cover the whole range of archival concerns, as earlier manuals attempted to do. If even basic issues of definition invite detailed study, then the authoritative manual of the future may turn out to be a goodly shelf long. It is much less clear that the basic issues have changed essentially, however. If archivists today, as in every generation, need to explore their world anew or in closer detail, they can nonetheless find strength and inspiration in the work of those who have gone before. Conservatism, in this sense, is not a matter of slavish adherence to precedent but an attempt to conserve those things of continuing value, since our collegiality as archivists engaged in a common endeavor extends across time.

Partly because of this conservative perspective, I have drawn only modestly on work done in areas often associated with archival studies. History will be used from time to time by way of example, as will law, diplomatics, and language studies. However, like the definitional work done by Schellenberg and Jenkinson, this study remains essentially archival and theoretical in approach. Though any number of conceptual issues facing archivists could doubtless be treated in like manner, a study of the nature of public records today readily invites a traditional method of treatment. This is true not just because of the size of the subject, but for deeper reasons connected with its very nature.

For one thing, different groups of people have different ideas about the nature of public records. This should come as no surprise. After all, documents are of deep importance to a number of professions, each with its own work and a correspondingly different view of the nature of records. Historians, in their search for evidence of the past, generally distinguish between written and unwritten sources, dividing the written ones into narrative or literary sources and non-narrative or record sources. They may or may not have archival considerations in mind when making such distinctions, but that is natural and all to the good; they have their own distinct concerns.[4]

The same holds for judges and lawyers, particularly in their concern over documentary evidence. The distinctions they draw between such things as public, official, and judicial documents may be confusing archivally, but they were hardly formulated for archival purposes.[5] What may be confusing to an archivist is no doubt clear to a judge. So, too, the special legal definition of records in the common law which, though important for archivists to know, remains a legal, not an archival, definition.[6] Legal definitions set down by legislators pose similar problems, for legislators also have their own particular concerns. Statutory laws, at whatever level of government, generally deal with specific subjects. They may define records, but often "for the purposes of this Act" alone, and such definitions rarely jibe with one another.[7] Archivists should, of course, know the legislation under which they work and will be bound by the particular definition of public records enacted in their jurisdiction. But such definitions can change, and archivists fortunate enough to contribute to those changes do well to bring their own point of view to the table. So, while existing legal definitions may bind them from day to day, archivists need not feel obliged to accept them as the sole foundation of their thinking—especially since they are usually made by others with their own distinct perspectives.[8]

These several definitions of records are natural and understandable. For archivists, though, they are like *faux amis,* words having the same spelling in English and French but possessing different meanings. We try to square them all at our peril. Consider, for example, the situation in England during the middle of the nineteenth century. At that time, it was not clear whether the recently created Public Record Office was to house only the Chancery's legal records or departmental records of all sorts. The term *records* had for centuries been associated with the legal definition, and archivists wanted to apply it to a wider range of material, but a clear distinction was not always drawn between the legal and archival definitions of records. As a result, some archivists attempted to twist the legal definition toward an archival one, but only got themselves tied up in knots.[9] Then there is the pioneering work of Holmes, who shows that statutory and case law definitions of public records are so much "brush and brambles" on the path toward an archival definition.[10] But this diversity of usage need not prove a barrier to clarity. If archivists and librarians can use the word *series* in different ways and not get confused, there is no reason why we should feel uncomfortable with definitions of public records set down by judges, legislators, historians, or even civil libertarians. Different contexts generate different meanings.[11]

The need to steer clear of potential *faux amis* suggests approaching the subject of public records with a minimum of borrowing from other areas. Even within the archival realm, however, there are good reasons for a strictly theoretical approach to the subject today. Among other things, the nature of public records is in some ways a hot topic. Questions regarding access to information, the right to privacy, and the proper disposition of ministerial and presidential papers have caused no end of debate. Any account of public records produced in such an atmosphere is bound to be affected by it in some way, especially the more empirical it attempts to be. Theoretical efforts are doubtless also affected, if perhaps in more subtle ways. But it seems reasonable to suppose that the closer a study remains to specific bodies of records, the more likely will it tend to gravitate toward issues surrounding those records.

Another reason for approaching the subject theoretically is that all archivists have ideas about the nature of public records. It would be surprising if they did not, for the concept is central to the profession. Archivists use it to a greater or lesser degree in most areas of archival work, including appraisal, acquisition, arrangement, description, and reference. They do so whether working in repositories housing public records, private records, or combinations of the two. All the same, they work with different kinds of institutional or personal documents, and their daily concerns naturally tend to draw their attention toward certain questions. A university archivist may puzzle over the public or private nature of faculty papers (or even which of them are in fact records) while his colleague in the legal archives across town may wonder whether judges really have a right to take their benchbooks home. To do justice to all the particular concerns that archivists have, a general account of public records that attempted to stay close to actual bodies of records would have to be impossibly broad in scope. Theory, on the other hand, has the merit of speaking by implication to all concerns, with far fewer words—at least in theory.

Perhaps, without pretending to exhaust the question, a final reason for the near necessity of a theoretical approach might be offered: many of us tend to define things by pointing to examples.[12] If asked what a cat is, for instance, one might reasonably point to the grey Persian here, the orange tabby there, and the white Siamese across the way. Some might think that North Americans, with their reputed pragmatism, are prone to this habit, and others might suspect that North American practitioners of an applied science might be even more so. In any event, the simple fact of experiencing the world moment by moment and thing by thing makes this tendency to define by examples quite natural. It might be recalled, in this regard, that Socrates was always bumping up against such answers among the Athenians, those supposedly archetypal theorists.

But this way of defining things is not the best initial approach toward understanding public records. For one thing, it would bog the discussion down by requiring the description of half the records that exist, at least if public and private may be assumed to exhaust the whole. Even more, though, it would not persuade, for at some point one must ask what all the examples have in common. What is it about the Persian, tabby, and Siamese that encourages us to apply the word *cat* to all of them? In the same way, an approach that asks directly what all public records have in common, starting perhaps with uncontroversial examples, may finally prove more practical and persuasive. At the very least, such efforts at theory offer a starting point for more refined theoretical discussions or other studies dealing more directly with particular bodies of records. Together, the many theoretical and empirical studies of public records may someday provide a full and satisfying account. At that point, of course, it will be time for the revisionists to provoke more and better thought.

Given the admittedly theoretical approach taken in this study, the view of archival theory that underlies it requires some clarification. Although no doubt implicit in the chapters dealing with records and public records, my assumptions about theory need setting forth at the outset, for two main reasons. First, as mentioned, North American archivists do not share a common view of archival theory. Second, the method employed may seem unorthodox to readers accustomed to a more empirical approach to archival questions. The possibilities for misunderstanding, given these factors, are legion. As a result, an attempt to share the assumptions under-lying this study seems opportune.

Chapter 1 accordingly sets the stage by exploring how the term *theory* has been used, both in common language and by archivists, and is followed in Chapter 2 by a discussion of the nature of archival theory. Employing the concept of theory developed in the first two chapters, the discussion of public records begins by ana-lyzing the concept of records in Chapter 3. This is followed by a logical bridge between the concepts of records and the public in the fourth chapter, which is in turn followed by an examination of the nature of public records in Chapter 5. The Appendix on access to information provides one example of how the concept of public records developed here can be applied to more specific issues.

NOTES

1. T. R. Schellenberg, *Modern Archives: Principles and Techniques* (Chi-cago: University of Chicago Press, 1956), pp. 15-16. The implication that the distinction between archives and records generally associated with Schellenberg has become obsolete will be found in the first definition of *archives* offered in Lewis J. Bellardo and Lynn Lady Bellardo, comps., *A Glossary for Archivists, Manuscript Curators, and Records Managers* (Chicago: Society of American Archivists, Archival Fundamentals Series, 1992), p. 3.

2. S. Muller, J. A. Feith, and R. Fruin, *Manual for the Arrangement and Description of Archives* (New York: H. W. Wilson, 1968), p. 9.

3. Hilary Jenkinson, *A Manual of Archive Administration* (London: Percy Lund, Humphries & Co., 1965), pp. 2-11; Schellenberg, *Modern Archives,* pp. 11-16; Muller, Feith, and Fruin, *Manual,* pp. 13-18.

4. See, for example, David C. Douglas and George W. Greenaway, eds., *English Historical Documents, 1042-1189* (London: Eyre & Spottiswoode, 1968), p. 11; and Bryce Lyon, *A Constitutional and Legal History of Medieval England,* 2nd ed. (New York: W. W. Norton, 1980), p. 3. Among those historians showing a particular sensitivity to archival concerns, one might note C. R. Cheney, "The Records of Medieval England," in his *Medieval Texts and Studies* (Oxford: Clarendon Press, 1973), p. 3; and G. R. Elton, *England, 1200-1640* (Ithaca, NY: Cornell University Press, The Sources of History, 1969), p. 137.

5. G. D. Nokes, *An Introduction to Evidence,* 4th ed. (London: Sweet and Maxwell, 1967), pp. 353-56, 432-42.

6. For an example of this common law definition, see Chapter 3.

7. Gary M. Peterson and Trudy Huskamp Peterson, *Archives and Manu-scripts: Law* (Chicago: Society of American Archivists, Basic Manual Series,

1985), p. 10. Oliver W. Holmes, "'Public Records'—Who Knows What They Are?" *American Archivist* 23 (January 1960): 6, 10. Interpretation acts may of course standardize definitions for particular jurisdictions, at least for some terms, but do not necessarily provide consistency across boundaries.

8. For a discussion of the relevance of archival definitions to the framing of legislation, see Victoria Bryans, "Towards an Integrated Approach to Public Records Legislation," paper presented at the 5th Canadian Records Management Conference, sponsored by ARMA and entitled "Black Gold '89: Capping the Information Explosion," Edmonton, Alberta, February 27 to March 2, 1989, pp. 3-7. Further discussion by the same author can be found in Victoria Lemieux, "Archival Solitudes: The Impact on Appraisal and Acquisition of Legislative Concepts of Records and Archives," *Archivaria* 35 (Spring 1993): 153-61.

9. For an example of an archivist laboring manfully, but with small success, to deal with Sir Edward Coke's influential common law pronouncements, see F. S. Thomas, *Notes of Materials for the History of Public Departments* (London, 1846), pp. 113-15. A sketch of the general confusion of terms can be found in the "Grigg Report," pp. 8-15 (Great Britain, Parliament, *Report of the Committee on Departmental Records*, Cmnd. 9163, July 1954). Outlines of the background are available in Peter Walne, "The Record Commissions, 1800-37," in *Prisca Munimenta: Studies in Archival & Administrative History Presented to Dr* [sic] *A.E.J. Hollaender*, ed. Felicity Ranger (London: University of London Press, 1973), pp. 9-18; and John Cantwell, "The 1838 Public Record Act and Its Aftermath: A New Perspective," *Journal of the Society of Archivists* 7 (April 1984): 277-86. A useful annotated bibliography can be found in Edgar B. Graves, ed., *A Bibliography of English History to 1485* (Oxford: Clarendon Press, 1975), pp. 110-18.

10. Holmes, "'Public Records,'" p. 26. Many readers thought he was in fact attempting to define the concept rather than clear away the obstacles, though Holmes denies this in "Remarks of Oliver W. Holmes," *American Archivist* 25 (April 1962): 238.

11. Civil libertarian concerns over access to information give a different twist to the notion of "public" records, as indeed do similar archival concerns. See, for example, British Columbia Civil Liberties Association, "Right to Public Information and the Protection of Individual Privacy" (Vancouver, 1985), and the Appendix to the present study. On the "insulating power of the context," see C. S. Lewis, *Studies in Words* (Cambridge: Cambridge University Press, 1960), pp. 8-14.

12. A typical instance of definition by examples occurs in the Canadian *Access to Information Act*, where the term *record* includes "any correspondence, memorandum, book, plan, map, drawing, diagram, pictorial or graphic work, photograph, film, microform, sound recording, videotape, [or] machine readable record" (*Revised Statutes of Canada* 1985, Ch. A-1, Sec. 3).

Chapter 1

Theory in Common Language and Archival Usage

THEORY IN COMMON LANGUAGE USAGE

Theory derives etymologically through Latin from the Greek "theoria," from "theoros," meaning "spectator," and "theoreo," meaning "behold." At its root is the concept of vision, of seeing and things seen. It is no accident that Plato presents his theory of knowledge through the metaphor of the light-giving sun, which enables us to perceive, see, or envision objects with varying degrees of reality. Clear perception of that theoria, he would argue, is a first step toward enlightenment, a true view of the real world. Many, however, would consider him a mere visionary.[1]

One finds, on reflection, that this root sense of the term remains in English. Leaving aside obsolete usage, three meanings that *theory* has had over the years in English can be usefully distinguished: a hypothesis; a programmatic scheme of ideas; and an explanatory scheme of ideas. Various tones of feeling have attached themselves over time to the words embodying these meanings. Williams, for instance, generally speaks of speculation rather than hypothesis and doctrine or ideology rather than a programmatic scheme of ideas.[2] This makes sense in a lexicological study requiring attention to actual quotations. For present purposes, I prefer to use what seem more neutral or positive terms (however ungainly some of them may be) in order to prejudge these meanings of theory as little as possible. It may be true that she dreams, you speculate, and I hypothesize. It may also be true that he is a slave to his ideology, you adhere to your doctrine, and I offer my program for consideration. In any case, all three of us engage in similar activities.

Unsurprisingly, considering the etymology of the term, and whatever the tone of feeling attached to them, all three of these meanings—hypothesis, program, and explanation—situate theory squarely within the realm of the mind. From all points of view, theory has been seen as something resulting from mental processes—be it ideas, concepts, beliefs, visions, or imaginings. This is only to say that theory is something we typically distinguish in common speech from two other things. We distinguish it from practice, since we can separate our thoughts about doing things from the things we do. "That makes sense in theory, but how will it work in practice?" We also distinguish theory from the nature of things, our thoughts about what exists being separable from what in fact exists. "That is certainly possible in theory, but is it really true?"

As facts about English language usage rather than philosophical claims, these common language distinctions between theory and action and between theory and the nature of things provide a useful means of examining the similarities and differences between the three meanings of the term outlined above. First of all, theory as hypothesis can relate to either things or actions. One can speculate, hypothesize, or dream about the nature of the universe, as well as about what persons do. "Everything is water," argued Thales. "The sun is a heavenly host of angels," said Blake. "We are brothers and sisters of the self-same earth," urged Socrates. In themselves, all these assertions are hypothetical claims of equal weight.

On reflection, it becomes clear that one can speculate or hypothesize not only about the nature of things and actions but also about their desirability or appropriateness. This point is perhaps clearest when the actual and the desirable are viewed in relation to human action, where the distinction often crops up in relation to the potential results of hypothesizing. Ethical and political systems, for example, are conceivable results of hypothesizing about the desirability of different possible courses of human action, whereas psychological or social models could result from speculation about what persons actually do. The distinction between the actual and the desirable is less instructive in relation to the nature of the world, largely because hypotheses about the desirability of the nature of the world as it exists do not fit readily with our usual ideas about what theory consists of. The most that might be said, perhaps, would be to urge that such hypotheses would seem to lead, at best, mainly to works of imagination, as opposed to hypotheses about the actual nature of things, which could result in scientific theories of various sorts. The latter are concerned more with the true than with the desirable. In short, one can hypothesize, speculate, or dream about virtually anything—about what exists or is desirable, about humanity or the world.

Theory, as a programmatic scheme of ideas, is more limited in scope than theory as hypothesis. Relating primarily to the field of human action, it does not deal with the nature or desirability of the world and is generally limited to the field of desirable, as opposed to actual, human behavior. In other words, theory of this sort is mainly about right and wrong, good and bad, appropriate and inappropriate actions. It is normative and practical, not descriptive and predictive. It aims not so much to describe what we actually do as to help us decide what we ought to do. It is theory from the actor's, the agent's, the practitioner's perspective. It consists, in one sense, of "a largely programmatic idea of how things should be," or, more precisely, of how things *human* should be; or, more precisely yet, of how the relations between persons and the circumstances they create could be, would most appropriately be, and should accordingly be moved toward.[3] In the broadest sense, theory of this sort embodies some idea of the good.

Unlike this second meaning of the term, theory as an explanatory scheme of ideas is concerned primarily with the actual. Theory of this sort—generally the meaning of the term used when speaking of science—can deal either with the nature of things or with the nature of human actions. But it is not usually associated with the attempt to determine what is appropriate. Whereas theory of the programmatic sort is normative and practical, assessing various possible courses of action and which among them is most desirable, this form of theory is descriptive, predictive, explanatory. It aims to describe and explain what we do and how the world works, rather than determine what we ought to do. It is theory from the observer's, not the actor's, point of view.[4]

Given these three common meanings of theory—hypothesis, program, and explanation—I think it best to limit the following discussion to the latter two. The main reason for doing so is that theory as hypothesis or speculation is too broad in scope and too limited in substance to contribute much besides confusion. This meaning of the term is too broad not only because it can apply to virtually everything, but more particularly because it applies to the differing areas covered by the other two meanings and is potentially encompassed by both. "Potentially" is an important qualifier here, for hypotheses have the interesting quality of either leading to programmatic or explanatory schemes of ideas or existing in wraithlike sterility. To come into full existence, to become something other than mere thought, all the potential results of speculation mentioned earlier depend on its elaboration, development, and testing. These potential results—such as models of political behavior, for example—are not hypothesis or speculation itself which, though doubtless a reasonably harmless activity, is basically a nonproductive form of theory. Unless it moves beyond itself, it bears no fruit. This holds true no matter what we choose to call this kind of theory. Whether he dreams or you hypothesize, there either can or cannot be tangible and substantive results, depending on whether and how he elaborates his dreams and you test your hypotheses. Theory of this sort, as it bears most directly on the present discussion, is largely a preliminary step toward the other two kinds of theory. It does not parallel them, and therefore will not be considered in what follows as a form of theory in its own right. But it will none-the-less lurk at the edges of the discussion, a dangerous sense of the term worth bearing in mind.

Setting aside hypothesis leaves us with theory as program and explanation. As noted, the former deals primarily with the area of appropriate action, whereas the latter deals mainly with the areas of actual human action and the actual nature of the world. The possible nature of the world has been set to one side as an area that does not concern theory (except in the dangerous sense), the products of speculation about it falling more typically into the area of imaginative works. These two common meanings of theory relate to different aspects of things, providing two different perspectives, the normative and the descriptive. The relations between these two perspectives will be considered presently. For now, it is enough to note that both sorts of theory deal with schemes of ideas and can therefore reasonably be considered two species of the same thing. Theory, in common usage, refers to an arrangement, array, scheme, or set of ideas, whether explanatory or programmatic.

THEORY IN ARCHIVAL USAGE

Theory has been a troublesome word for North American archivists of late. Some say that it does not or cannot exist. Others, warning their colleagues against pretentious attempts at "high-falutin' archival theory," consider it either "myth or banality." Still others see it extending into the realm of metaphysics.[5] Given this diversity of usage and the colorful language in which some of these claims have been couched, the authors of a recent archival lexicon were perhaps prudent to omit the term from their compilation.[6] Clearly, an examination of some representative meanings of theory in archival usage is warranted.

Most recent archival discussions of theory follow from Frank Burke's 1981 article, in which theory is defined as "universal laws immutable and applicable at all times, in all places."[7] Such laws result from hypotheses framed in universal form, tested against the evidence, and found valid. This definition exemplifies the common meaning of theory as an explanatory scheme of ideas. For Burke, this type of theory is not simply to be distinguished from the practical, normative, programmatic form of theory, but stands opposed to it. "Pure theory has no relation to action," he argues. "If it did, it would be a plan or a process, not a theory."[8] Theory, then, does not deal with "the mundane matters of arrangement and description, the techniques of microfilming or lamination, the dendritical structure of organizational records," and so forth. It deals rather with "the larger questions," such as the nature of organizations and organizational decision making, historiography, the motives for creating records and revering artifacts, and the purpose of archives in society.[9] Burke does not explore the relations between these various areas of theoretical investigation or clarify how they would fit into his characterization of archival theory. It is even difficult to discern his reasons for believing that studies of organizations, social psychology, or historiography could lead to universal and immutable laws. I say this not so much by way of criticism as to note that Burke seems primarily concerned with encouraging the study of new areas. After all, he finds that little if any such theory exists. He offers an ideal of archival theory, in other words, a vision of what he would like to see, not an analysis of what exists.[10] He calls for university programs for archivists, drawing an ideal portrait of the sort of theory that he thinks would be acceptable in that environment.[11] The resulting view of archival theory envisions studies leading toward an explanatory scheme of ideas that places the daily concerns of archivists within a broad social, psychological, and historical framework.

John Roberts, writing partly in response to Burke, examines the concept of archival theory largely in terms of a general distinction between theory and practice, in which practice is what archivists do and theory is what they think (and write) about what they do.[12] Accordingly, he begins by positing two strains of archival theory. The first one, having to do with "the nuts and bolts or craft aspects" of archival work, he does not consider genuinely theoretical. Here echoing Burke, he dismisses methodological works concerning such "mundane matters" as arrangement and description from the realm of genuine theory because they represent "simply a codification of craftsmanship." He also dismisses more abstract principles, such as provenance, on the grounds that "ultimately, they have to do with organization, categorization, and retrieval, and hence are largely practical tools." The second strain of archival thinking, or theory, identified by Roberts relates to historiography. He argues that "knowledge of historical scholarship and of the content of particular collections become the essential components in making informed, professional decisions about appraisal, description, and reference." This type of theory, he claims, is not archival but historical.[13]

The two kinds of archival theory thus identified are brought together in the following argument: if one kind is archival but not theoretical, and the other is theoretical but not archival, then archival theory per se does not really exist. This argument is not entirely clear as it stands, because applied historiography, as Roberts characterizes it, is ultimately as much "about practice" as is the methodological type of archival theory, since it is to be used to make decisions regarding archival work. Therefore, it too is not genuinely theoretical in his sense. In fact, all the forms of archival thinking that he identifies must be "about practice" in some sense, since all thinking about what archivists do (to borrow the terms of his assumed distinction between theory and practice) relates by definition to what they do. To say this is not to refute his argument but only to suggest that it be rephrased as follows: if one type of archival theory is archival but not theoretical, and the other type is neither archival nor theoretical, then archival theory per se does not really exist.

Like Burke, Roberts claims that genuine theory does not have any relation to practical matters. Unlike Burke, however, he claims that *archival* theory can pertain to nothing else.[14] Accordingly, while Burke locates archival theory within the category of theory as explanation, Roberts locates it within the category of theory as program. Real, true, genuine theory is, for him, of the explanatory sort—like the theoretical formulations of physics—whereas archival theory is practical, normative, programmatic. Therefore, what he calls archival theory is not "theoretical" by his definition of the term. Believing that real theory deals with important matters, Roberts denies archival thinking the full meaning of the word *theoretical* because he considers "high-falutin' archival theory...a rather superfluous and unpromising diversion."[15] Real theory deals with important matters in an explanatory way; archival thinking does not.

The persuasiveness of this argument is not the point at issue here. What is important to note is that Roberts' normative, practice-related definition of archival theory adds a second meaning to the one offered by Burke. This meaning of archival theory is, in fact, widely represented in English language writings over the past several generations, although few commentators have doubted its usefulness or validity. Jenkinson, for example, distinguishes archival theory from practice or practical matters, theory relating to "matters of principle" and practice to the application of those principles in daily archival work. For him, principles are to be applied "as criteria of correct procedure." Archival theory, as he views it, applies to archival work across geographical boundaries. It is thus universal in Burke's sense, at least within a given era, and pertains directly to practical work.[16] Schellenberg does not use the term *theory* as readily as Jenkinson does. Instead, he refers mainly to "principles and techniques," by which he seems to distinguish essentially what Jenkinson refers to as theory and practice: general ideas about various aspects of archival work, as distinct from the means (or techniques) of applying those general ideas (or principles) in practice.[17] In a similar manner, Posner liked to call himself an "archival theorist or generalist." He was a teacher and writer, as opposed to a practitioner, one who observes and describes in terms of general ideas rather than one who acts with reference to daily circumstances, applying those general ideas.[18] The theoretical and practical aspects of archival work are also distinguished in a recent popular book, in which it is suggested that archivists "base their actions and judgments on a framework of ideas," applying those ideas to an often disorderly reality. As a result of this distinction, the authors conclude that archival administration is "a blend of the abstract and the concrete, the theoretical and the practical."[19] Theory and practice, principles and techniques, thinking and doing — whatever the nuances, all these related distinctions serve as a common backdrop to the often employed notion of archival theory as normative and programmatic ideas.

A third representative use of *theory* in archival writing relates the term to purpose or meaning. It has been suggested, for instance, that archivists' practical activities should be based on "a sound theoretical even 'philosophical' footing, and on a sense of 'spiritual identity' which is infused with ethical and moral concerns as well as that sense of vision or mission that rises above (and raised [sic] up the significance of) the daily, the mundane, and the practical to give our work meaning."[20] This use of the term includes, but gives a twist to, the sense of archival theory as ideas applied in practice. If the more common normative, practical meaning relates to ideas that give archivists a sense of what they should do in their daily work, of what ideas they should employ, this sense of the term refers explicitly to the broader social meaning or purpose of that work. It does not directly answer the practitioner's question, "Why should I do the work according to these particular concepts?" The answer to that question, one may assume, is part of the argument— indeed, the rationale—for employing certain ideas in daily work. The answer to the practitioner's question would, in this view, take the following form: "Such and such ideas should be employed, yes; and they should be employed because it is reasonable to do so, given factors x, y, and z." The sense of archival theory as ideas embodying purpose relates, rather, to a question of a different order, the question of why one should bother doing the work at all. What relevance does it have? What use is it all? What does it *mean?* Above, beyond, or behind the concept of archival theory as ideas guiding practice is the notion of theory as ideas placing archival work within an acceptable scheme of values, ideals, or purposes. Doing so gives archivists a sense of dignity or worth in the world, something that makes sense within the society in which they ply their trade. Even more, such ideas provide archivists with an overall sense of direction, a "mission", as it were, based on their sense of where and how they fit into the larger scheme of things. Ideas of this sort provide both a sense of identity and a basis for action. Here, then, is a second sense in which "archival theory" is used normatively.

Attempting, in part, to clarify and synthesize earlier discussions, Frederick Stielow begins his ambitious essay on archival theory by defining it as "the codification of rational and systematic thinking, the conscious development of general principles or guides to explain or analyze."[21] As it stands, this definition most closely resembles Burke's, in so far as it exemplifies the common view of theory as a scheme of explanatory ideas. Although this is but a starting point for Stielow, drawn from a dictionary by way of convenience, a word of caution about dictionary definitions might be useful at this point. Dictionaries can provide a variety of definitions drawn from various sources and times. Because of this variety, such definitions give us only a sense of how words have been used, not an analysis of what they mean or how they can best be applied in any given circumstance. Borrowing a definition from a dictionary does not answer questions but provides the reader with a sense of the author's assumptions or intended direction.[22] Stielow, in other words, has chosen one of several possible places to begin.

Stielow begins with an explanatory definition because he takes Burke's article as his starting point. He criticizes what he takes to be Burke's call for "an exclusively scientific methodology," attempting to show that hypothesis building and empirical testing may be valid methods of developing archival theory but are not the only methods available.[23] The description and prediction of phenomena, he suggests, can be supplemented by historical analysis along the lines urged by Roberts, although he cautions that "the extent to which historiography can be adapted to govern archival matters is nothing more than a hypothesis to be tested over time." Nonetheless, he sees history as "the methodological bedrock for appraisal and documentation strategies" and reiterates his belief in the "value of historical scholarship" for archival work. Drawing together the scientific and historical approaches, Stielow argues that "archives is by definition a *metadiscipline*. It provides services at a level above (meta) specific issues or disciplines and whose theory is synthetic and expansive, embracing elements from both the humanities and science."[24]

Although he uses terms such as *theory, methodology,* and *scholarship* somewhat confusingly here, Stielow seems to be claiming that archival theory, as an explanatory scheme of ideas, can take either scientific or humanistic forms. This seems a reasonable interpretation, in that he goes on to argue for a programmatic component or form of archival theory as well, which "augments humanistic and scientific analysis." This form of theory—or component of the archival metadiscipline—consists of organizational theory. It stresses "control and prescription" as opposed to description, using "'science' as an instrument of improvement."[25] Stielow refers to this element of archival thought as *applied* theory, or as supplying an applied context for all forms of archival theory. However, the exact relations he sees between this normative species of theory and the explanatory sorts he has already discussed are not spelled out at length. Rounding out this part of his discussion, Stielow offers critical social theory as a fourth "theoretical school," which can provide archival thought with a means of reflective self-analysis by countering the tendency of applied thought to "support the political status quo uncritically."[26] Here, as with the discussion of organizational theory, not much elaboration is provided, so the exact relations Stielow envisages between this and other areas, forms, or "schools" of archival theory remain somewhat cloudy. Still, his emphasis on ethical considerations would seem to place this sort of archival theory in the normative category.

To a certain extent, the four kinds or forms of archival theory discussed by Stielow are drawn together in the final section of his article, "Toward a General Theory or Mission Statement." When speaking of archives as a metadiscipline, Stielow argued that "a distinct knowledge base for archives" would emerge, along with a shared understanding of what archivists are about. Drawing on F. S. C. Northrop, he urged that "a field's identity must be based first 'with [sic] the peculiar character of its particular problem.'" For Stielow, the "particular problem" for archivists is "the control, delivery, and preservation of manmade information, especially primary sources with enduring value."[27] Given this definition of the archivist's field of activity and the four kinds of theory already mentioned, he steps back and offers a fifth kind of archival theory that encompasses all the others while charting "a distinctive territory." This is what he refers to as a general theory or mission statement, which has three objects: to aid in codifying current knowledge, guide research and practice, and control biases.

The general theory, as I understand it, combines a description of the overall field with a general statement of the archivist's "responsibility for solutions to the archival problems" that make up the overall field.[28] Here Stielow is offering a normative definition of archival theory akin to the one mentioned above concerning the meaning or purpose of archival work. Archivists, he says, have two general responsibilities. The first is "to serve their institution and its mission through the management of primary information, especially that of enduring value." The second is "to the materials in their charge and to insure the development of a documentary heritage from these." As a corollary, he argues that archivists also have a responsibility "to improve their knowledge and services, especially in regard to their role as intermediaries in the archival information process and the continuum between their sources and users." In offering this normative definition of archival theory, Stielow combines a view of what archivists do, who they are, and how they should go about their work — a sense of identity and a basis for reasoned and principled action.

Whether or not (or to what degree) one agrees with Stielow's overall view is less important than an understanding of the ways in which he speaks of archival theory. As mentioned above, his use of terms such as *methodology* and *scholarship* are somewhat confusing, at least when they are taken as referring to what he considers different species of theory. Scholarship, for instance, is generally considered a result or kind of "rational and systematic thinking" that can take many different forms. As such, it is broader than theory as "the codification of" such thinking, as in Stielow's first definition. *Methodology* generally refers to a means of gaining knowledge, of making sure that thinking is indeed rational and systematic, as well as any codification that may follow it. No doubt the codification of rational and systematic thinking *about the means of* gaining or codifying that thinking can be considered an aspect of theory, as well. Still, to speak of the two in the same breath makes for some difficulty.

These comments should not be construed as criticism. They are made simply by way of attempting to determine precisely what it is that Stielow means when speaking of archival theory — what it is about archival theory that enables him to include all his various definitions of it in a single article. The difficulties just mentioned point toward his intended meaning, which is the common archival use of *theory* noted earlier: the whole of archivists' thinking about their work, as distinguished from the work itself. No precise distinctions need be made among methodology, scholarship and theory when all of them are included in the general category of archival thought. Stielow's discussion of the discipline of archives and its relation to his first four definitions of archival theory supports such an interpretation. This, after all, is a discipline that provides "services" through scholarship and methodology, while having an organizational component (or form of theory or type of theory or applied perspective) as well as including a "school" of critical thought.

What this all means is not entirely clear until one realizes that *discipline* is used to refer to the whole range of archival work, not just to a distinct area of study, as the term is often used. No precise distinctions need be made between the theoretical components of this discipline when all of them are essentially forms of thinking about the work that archivists do. Stielow's discussion remains consistent when he considers general theory, in that it draws together all components of archival thinking as parts of an overall mission for archivists. The various types of archival theory all fit together, insofar as they all contribute toward the same end. While taking a step beyond the common definition of archival theory as archival thinking by placing it within a general framework, Stielow offers several components of that thinking. As a result, he offers two programmatic or purposive definitions of archival theory. One pertains to the whole of archival thinking, as opposed to archival practice; the other pertains to the purpose of that thought. These two notions of archival theory, brought together by Stielow in an original way, are the same as the two normative uses of the term already discussed.

As used by archivists, then, *theory* has taken on a number of different meanings that fall within the common meanings of theory as explanatory or programmatic ideas. Broadly speaking, three meanings have been distinguished in the foregoing discussion. Two of these archival uses of the term are programmatic or normative in one way or another. Most commonly, archival theory refers to archivists' thinking about their work, as contrasted with archival practice or the work itself. This meaning of the term is programmatic in the most general sense, in that it covers the whole of archival thought, which is assumed to be directed toward achieving, understanding, or improving archival practice. The second normative meaning of the term pertains to the overall purpose or meaning of archival work. In this sense, *theory* refers to a more specific kind of thought about archival work than the former use of the term. It has a different, more focused aim and a different level of application, being concerned with directing archival work (and thinking) as a whole through an understanding of the general identity and goals of archivists. The third meaning of *theory* is explanatory rather than normative in nature. In this sense of the term, archival theory refers to ideas that describe and explain the facts available to archivists for understanding their distinctive field of scientific inquiry.

NOTES

1. For the etymology of *theory* see Eric Partridge, *Origins: A Short Etymological Dictionary of Modern English,* 2nd ed. (New York: Macmillan, 1959), s.v. "Theater," para. 4, pp. 710-11; and Joseph T. Shipley, *Dictionary of Word Origins* (Totowa, NJ: Littlefield, Adams & Co., 1967), s.v. "Spoonerism," p. 333. An example of Plato's use of the sun metaphor is found in *The Republic of Plato* (London: OUP, 1941), pp. 218-32 [VI. 507-VII. 518].

2. See Raymond Williams, *Keywords: A Vocabulary of Culture and Society* (London: Fontana/Croom Helm, 1976), pp. 266-68. A wide array of historical examples from which Williams draws will be found in *The Oxford English Dictionary,* 2nd ed. (Oxford: Clarendon Press, 1989), 13: 902.

3. Williams, *Keywords,* p. 267.

4. The differences between the descriptive and normative perspectives as they relate to political behavior are discussed in Joseph Tussman, *Obligation and the Body Politic* (London: Oxford University Press, 1960), pp. 12-16.

5. Frank G. Burke, "The Future Course of Archival Theory In the United States," *American Archivist* 44 (Winter 1981): 40-46; John W. Roberts, "Archival Theory: Much Ado About Shelving," *American Archivist* 50 (Winter 1987): 74; Terry Cook, "ACA Conference Overview," *ACA Bulletin* 12 (July 1988): [3-4]. See also Frank G. Burke, "In Defense of Archival Theory, or Pinkett's Last Charge!" paper presented at the 52nd Annual General Meeting of the Society of American Archivists, Atlanta, Georgia, Septem-

ber 30, 1988; and John W. Roberts, "Archival Theory: Myth or Banality?" *American Archivist* 53 (Winter 1990): 110-20.

6. Bellardo and Bellardo, *A Glossary for Archivists, Manuscript Curators, and Records Managers.*

7. Burke, "The Future Course of Archival Theory in the United States," p. 42. Actually, he speaks of theory as *the development of* such laws. However, by this I understand him to mean the activity of theorizing, as opposed to the laws that result from it, which would be theory proper in his sense of the term. Hence the truncated quotation.

8. Ibid., p. 40.

9. Ibid., pp. 42-44.

10. Ibid., p. 42.

11. Ibid., pp. 44-46.

12. Roberts, "Archival Theory: Much Ado About Shelving." Although he generally tends to refer to theory as the literature on archival practice, as opposed to archivists' thinking about that practice, whether published or not, Roberts' claim that certain theoretical questions "can be asked and competently answered by any archivist" (p. 73) suggests that the opposition between thinking and doing presents a just characterization of his view.

13. Ibid., pp. 68-69.

14. In his "Archival Theory: Myth or Banality?" Roberts depicts a third strain of archival theory pertaining to archivists' borrowing from other disciplines. Although he would seem to find less worth in some of these areas than in historiography, the tenor of his hypotheses suggests that this kind of theory can be included, for the sake of argument, within the second category of archival theory, the nonarchival and nontheoretical.

15. Roberts, "Archival Theory: Much Ado About Shelving," p. 74.

16. Jenkinson, *A Manual of Archive Administration*, pp. xii, 19. See also his appendix outlining a "Catalogue of the Ideal Library for an Archivist," in which the section on archival theory pertains to custody, care, arrangement, and publication. The other sections deal respectively with printed guides to existing archives, administrative history, publications containing archival material, and works in the interpretive sciences such as diplomatics, paleography, and sigillography (pp. 198-205).

17. See, for instance, his *Modern Archives*, which includes such chapter headings as Classification Principles, Disposition Practices, Principles of Arrangement, and Description Practices.

18. Ernst Posner, "The National Archives and the Archival Theorist," in his *Archives and the Public Interest: Selected Essays by Ernst Posner*, ed. Ken Munden (Washington, DC: Public Affairs Press, 1967), pp. 131, 140.

19. Maygene F. Daniels and Timothy Walch, eds., *A Modern Archives Reader: Basic Readings on Archival Theory and Practice* (Washington, DC: National Archives and Records Service, 1984), p. xi.

20. Cook, "ACA Conference Overview," p. 3. See also Kent M. Haworth, "The Principles Speak for Themselves: Articulating a Language of Purpose for Archives," in Barbara L. Craig, ed., *The Archival Imagination: Essays in Honour of Hugh A. Taylor* (Ottawa: Association of Canadian Archivists, 1992), pp. 90-104. There is also a strong element of this sense of theory in Burke's call for study of the purpose of archives in society, as discussed above.

21. Frederick J. Stielow, "Archival Theory Redux and Redeemed: Definition and Context Toward a General Theory," *American Archivist* 54 (Winter 1991): 17.

22. Given this distinction between usage and meaning, the fruitlessness of looking up a word in a dictionary when disagreement arises over what a term means, or should mean, becomes readily apparent. To seek the one authoritative dictionary in which to look would, of course, only compound the error.

23. Stielow, "Archival Theory Redux and Redeemed," pp. 18-19.

24. Ibid., p. 21 and note 30 at the same place.

25. Ibid., p. 22.

26. Ibid., pp. 23, 25.

27. Ibid., p. 22.

28. Ibid., pp. 23-24.

Chapter 2

Theory as Used in the Present Study

My own view of archival theory does not diverge in principle from the definitions explored above. Indeed, it not only draws on those definitions but, where it differs, does little more than combine, distinguish between, elaborate on, or emphasize elements of them. It would be foolish to pretend otherwise, for all discussions of archival theory must deal with the same fundamental reality, and I make no claim to having seen more of that reality than my colleagues. However, there are some differences in the view of archival theory offered here, as there obviously are between those already described. Rather than attempt to spell out all the various similarities and differences or evaluate these other views of theory comprehensively, the following pages mainly explain my own position. Therefore, while other definitions of theory will be further explored to some extent, no attempt will be made to examine each of them thoroughly or work out all the nuances of their interrelations. They will serve, rather, as reference points within a basically self-contained exposition.

In common usage, theory is most clearly understood as a scheme of ideas, whether normative or explanatory. It is a form of knowledge, conceptual in nature. This, in broad outline, is the definition of theory adopted in the present study. Archival theory is neither nonexistent, high-falutin', mythical, banal, nor metaphysical. It consists, rather, of organized conceptual knowledge resulting from the analysis of basic archival ideas. No mystery lies hidden here. Analysis involves examining the meaning of an idea or concept, attempting to determine what it is—its nature, what it amounts to—the same activity that Socrates was engaged in when asking for definitions.[1] Basic archival ideas, the focus of analysis, concern the nature of such things as archives, records, fonds, and so forth. They are "basic" in the sense that other ideas or concepts are based on them, so archival theory as a whole can be characterized within a logical framework of ideas and their relations.[2] The activity is theorizing; the result, theory.

From this perspective, the chapters in this book dealing with records and public records exemplify what I mean both by analysis and by the relations between basic and secondary concepts. What I mean by organized conceptual knowledge is best approached by using this view of archival theory to explore the outlines of several central issues in relation to the overall image of the archival endeavor that it engenders. Accordingly, the remainder of this chapter examines the relations between theory and practice, between theoretical and empirical knowledge, and between the descriptive and normative perspectives within archival theory. While clarifying the view of theory adopted in this study and demonstrating its utility, the examination of these issues will provide a broad outline of the nature of archival work and the role of theory within it.

THEORY AND PRACTICE

The most common view of archival theory discussed earlier—archival thinking as a whole—is both useful and problematic. Its usefulness is evident from the very popularity it has had over the years. This is as it should be, for one of the constants of the archival endeavor is the fact that archivists are both thinkers and doers, professionals involved in an applied field of work. To speak of theory as archivists' thinking about their work, in contrast to the work itself, makes good sense, simply because it reflects that reality.

However, while useful in characterizing two broad aspects of the archival endeavor, this apparently straightforward distinction between theory and practice has definite limitations. For one thing, it stretches the meaning of *theory* to the extent of making it synonymous with "thought." By doing so, this notion does not necessarily level all archival thinking, minimizing the possibility of distinguishing between different kinds of archival thought in a principled way. It still remains possible to speak of as many species of theory or thought as archivists may wish to enumerate. Still, this manner of speaking does deprive archivists of using *theory* to refer to one specific kind of thought among others, setting them apart from most other English speakers. Whether or not it may be bad in itself, this idiosyncratic usage by archivists nonetheless results in a degree of confusion at times, as when it becomes necessary to speak of empirical studies and scholarship in general as kinds of theory.[3] Aside from possible confusion, a related result of such usage—to be required to speak, for example, of the empirical as a species of the theoretical—is that archivists deprive themselves of an existing and respectable distinction between theoretical and other forms of thought embedded in English usage. The meaning of the term *theoretical* as conceptual knowledge becomes lost to archivists.

Another limitation of this distinction between theory and practice, at least if one takes it as fundamental, is its tendency to dichotomize thinking and doing. Every distinction runs the risk of implying unbreachable separation because it invites us to hold two concepts in mind, however they may in fact relate to each other. But there is a real hazard in the present case, since the unqualified notion of theory as something distinct from practice tends to falsely elevate or lower the status of both thought and action. If, for example, one claims that the development of theory will lead to a division of labor between theorists and practitioners (or theologians and parish priests, as Burke provocatively phrases it), the possibility of invidious comparison inevitably arises.[4] Others may be expected to react accordingly, especially if there is any suggestion that theory is somehow above or more important than practice. Claims that theory is nonexistent, banal, or presumptuous — that theorists are benighted fools and practitioners the salt of the earth—will likely not be far behind. Peacemakers may then appear, offering wise advice drawn from experience in related fields about the potentially disastrous results of building needless walls.[5]

Divisiveness of this sort is not only unattractive but unnecessary. Deriving from a distinction assumed to be a split, it grossly underestimates the complex relations that actually exist between theory and practice, complexities that begin to emerge clearly when theory is viewed as conceptual knowledge. From this point of view, the contrast between theory and practice amounts essentially to a distinction between ideas and their practical application.[6] Archivists, one might say, both have and use ideas. They do their everyday work in certain ways because of the ideas they hold about the nature of the material they work with.

For example, when arranging records, archivists attempt to maintain the order of documents originally given them by their creators, while at the same time respecting their provenance by refraining from mixing documents deriving from the activities of more than one creator. The precepts underlying this archival activity are generally referred to as the principles of provenance and original order. They form two aspects of the archival method of arrangement which archivists follow because they hold certain ideas about the nature of an organic body of records or fonds. In fact, it is these ideas about fonds that draw together two apparently discrete principles into a single method. This conjunction becomes clear when one asks why documents should be arranged according to provenance and original order. What is it about archives that requires a certain method of dealing with them?

One might begin to answer this question by pointing out that there are essentially two ways of looking at a fonds. One can look at it either as a whole, with its constituent parts, or as the interconnected parts that make up the whole. In a homey way, it recalls the old philosophical question: how is the one within the many, and how are the many part of the one? Looking at the whole, one realizes that a fonds is not an arbitrary creation but something with an independent existence deriving from the independent existence of its creator. At the same time, this body of documents was used in the course of an activity. The person or agency was a living thing, carrying out certain functions according to its particular nature and producing the documents as a result. In order to fulfill those functions, various activities had to be undertaken, and those activities were carried out through various particular transactions. As a result, the structure of the parts articulates the functions, activities, and actions of the whole. Hence the need to follow provenance, to keep the whole together, separate from other fonds, according to its creator.

A complementary formulation results when one asks how the many are part of the one—how the documents, files, and series are part of the fonds. Recalling that the fonds was once a living thing, one notices that the documents that make it up have some special relations with one another, and that it is the relations between the documents that make them "add up" to a particular fonds. One cannot simply say that keeping the fonds together as a whole will preserve the context in which the documents were created or used and then proceed to arrange them in an arbitrary way within the fonds. The order in which the documents were created expresses the nature of the transactions of which they formed a part. As Jenkinson says, they have "a structure, an articulation and a natural relationship between [them], which are essential to their significance."[7] These relations—necessary, determined, intrinsic, and originary—exist between documents within a file, files within a series, and series within the whole.[8] All together, they define the various functional levels within the fonds and express the organic quality of the whole. A second imperative, maintaining the original order, thus combines with the need to maintain provenance as a complementary and necessary aspect of a single archival method deriving from the nature of the documents.

That, at any rate, is one view of the matter.[9] Archivists may not always be conscious of such ideas while employing them to arrange documents, or in any other aspect of their work. Indeed, the most effective practice results from the use of ideas so well understood that they can be employed without self-consciousness, as part of an educated archivist's mindset. On the other hand, thinking too much of basic ideas while working, rather than with them, can cripple, like a golfer on the course thinking too much about hitting the ball instead of trusting the "instincts" developed on the practice tee. In addition to not necessarily being conscious of the ideas they use, archivists do not always set them up for examination. This is hardly surprising. After all, except for rare moments, who has the time? Nonetheless, it can be argued that archivists' concepts do, in fact, guide their practice at almost every turn.

There are two interrelated claims here that require clarification: ideas *always and inevitably* underlie archival practice; and this is true whether or not practice is recognized as the concrete expression of such ideas through their application. These claims may appear radical at first glance, particularly if ideas or concepts are equated too readily and directly with theory in the sense of conceptual knowledge. On closer examination, however, they turn out to be somewhat commonplace.

Consider the words of John Austin, who makes his case in terms of the basic distinction between theory and practice.

> They who talk of theory as if it were the antagonist of practice, or of a thing being true in *theory* but not true in *practice*, mean (if they have a meaning) that the theory in question is false; that the particular truths which it concerns are treated imper-

fectly or incorrectly; and that, if it were applied in practice, it might, therefore, mislead. They say that truth in theory is not truth in practice. They mean that a false theory is not a true one, and might lead us to practical errors.[10]

Austin's argument may be viewed as a counterpoint to the old German saying that "theory is what should work but doesn't; practice is what works but you don't know why."[11] From Austin's perspective, this saying should be rephrased as follows: "false theory is what should work but doesn't; true theory is what does work, whether or not you know why." The important claim here is that theory (true or false) always underlies practice, whether we are aware of it or not. The difficulty one may have in accepting this claim at face value—and the reason, perhaps, that thinkers like Austin find themselves having to make the argument time and again—lies mainly in its ambiguous use of the term *theory*. If this term is taken one way, the argument can only be partly sustained. If taken another way, however, the argument is both uncontroversial and sound.

If Austin means to argue that theory—in the sense of full-blown conceptual knowledge—always and inevitably underlies practice, then his argument cannot be fully sustained. Theory of this sort, if worthy to be considered knowledge in any substantial sense, must be both developed and articulated. In order to be recognized as conceptual knowledge, it must be available for examination or testing in some intellectually acceptable way. It seems fair to assume, if one is dealing with *conceptual* knowledge, that such examination requires not only an argument with some logically recognizable structure but an argument potentially available for public analysis, as well. Undeveloped concepts, as discussed earlier with regard to *theory* in common usage, may be classed as hypothesis or speculation, but can be considered theory only in the dangerous sense of the term. At the same time, the very process of developing concepts in this way implies awareness of them, entailing some degree of articulation, since otherwise one would have no means of determining what was being developed, in what way it was being developed, or even that such development was taking place or had in fact occurred. In other words, we cannot know without knowing that we know, and thereby be capable of sharing it, at least with regard to conceptual knowledge or theory in the full meaning of the term.

If this is the sense in which he uses *theory*, then Austin's argument cannot be fully sustained, because practice does not always employ developed and articulated conceptual knowledge. It was Plato's fond belief that the world, as he understood it, will be set to rights only when philosophers become kings or kings become philosophers. He may or may not be right, but I would venture that his ghost, walking abroad today, might not be entirely convinced that the day had yet arrived. For everyday purposes, at least, we are often well served by intuition, feelings, hunches, habits, imitation, and directives. In some cases, we may indeed act on developed and articulated concepts — as when, for example, an archivist employs a theory of the fonds such as that outlined above in arranging documents. But this is certainly not inevitably or invariably true.

If, however, Austin is using *theory* in the dangerous sense of hypothesis or speculation, then his argument is both obvious and sound. It amounts to a claim that because practitioners have minds, practice is not a mindless activity. This remarkably banal assertion is obscured by the common distinction between theory and practice taken to be a dichotomy between thinking and doing — a dichotomy also implied by the very language in which Austin couches his claim. Separating thinking from doing and thinkers from doers invites us to assume that concepts somehow exist only when fully developed and consciously set up for examination. In other words, our almost universal experience of doing things without simultaneously thinking about those things — without self-consciously reflecting on them — is maneuvered toward an intuitive sense that somehow we do not think and do at the same time.

This is true enough if by *thinking* we are referring exclusively to fully developed ideas consciously held in mind. However, we also use *thinking* in a looser sense to refer to holding ideas of any sort in mind. "I was just thinking about you," for instance, reflects something more akin to consciousness or awareness of the idea of that person than to reflection on a logically articulated concept. It is important to recognize, moreover, that such consciousness or awareness may not fully exist until the question is posed. When we know something, we may know that we know it. When we intuit, sense, or feel something, we often hold an idea in mind only in the sense of holding it in solution, available for awareness if needs be. From this perspective, it is reasonable to view the intuitions and hunches that often serve us from day to day as forms of thought accompanying action—more precisely, as indicators of thought underlying action. If so, then theory (in the dangerous sense, at least) can be said to underlie practice in all cases, simply because we have minds and ideas are the instruments by means of which the mind invariably functions. This is not to say that all activity involves grand ideas, organized ideas, articulated ideas, or even recognizable ideas. It is to say, however, that concepts of some sort always inform action, whether one is ordering a pizza or arranging documents according to accepted archival principles. Accordingly, if this is the sense in which Austin uses *theory*, then his argument is both commonplace and sound.

If nothing else, this explication of the ambiguity in Austin's argument serves to show that theorists who claim that theory inevitably underlies practice are to some extent playing with words. My own sense, however, is that they do have a point, although it may be lost when the argument is packed up in pithy phrases. What looks from one perspective like an ambiguous use of the term *theory* can also be viewed as something of a portmanteau argument in which certain connections between two meanings of a term disappear from view when packed together in a single spelling. With regard to archival work, at least, three elements are missing: the notion of methodology as intermediary between theory and practice; the continuum that exists between undeveloped and fully developed ideas; and the relationship between this continuum and the various levels of awareness of concepts. A brief exploration of each of these elements will give some indication of how far theory can reasonably be said to invariably underlie archival practice, whether one is aware of it or not.

First of all, the unqualified distinction between archival theory and practice allows no room for acknowledging the special position of methodology in archival work. Consider, for example, the concept of the fonds outlined above and its relation to the principles of provenance and original order. Archivists indeed have ideas about the nature of the material with which they work, such as the fonds. Those particular ideas, in turn, imply subsidiary ideas about how to work with the material, such as the principles of provenance and original order. These latter ideas concerning *how* to treat the material can also be analyzed in their own right, and for that reason it may be tempting to think of them as theoretical. However, such analysis can only be effective and complete when done in relation to the more fundamental concepts from which they derive. For the sake of clarity, they can be distinguished from the ideas about *what* the material is by calling them methodological. One can then speak of theory, methodology, and practice. For example, the methodology for arranging documents derives from the theory about the nature of an organic body of records, and archivists employ that methodology when actually applying the theory to a particular body of records. Methodology thus instrumentalizes theory, drawing it from the level of abstraction and harnessing it toward concrete results in the world, a Janus-faced intermediary between what at times seem the two solitudes of theorist and practitioner.[12] From this perspective, Austin's argument needs to be qualified as follows.

> They who talk of theory as if it were the antagonist of practice, or of a thing being true in *theory* but not true in *practice*, mean (if they have a meaning) that the theory in question is false— *or that the methodology used to employ it in practice was derived in a faulty manner or employed inadequately.*

Recognizing the intermediary position of methodology in relation to theory and practice reveals a degree of complexity in the argument hidden by the ambiguous use of *theory.*

Another element missing from the argument concerns the continuum existing between undeveloped and fully developed ideas. As noted, a useful distinction can be made between theory as a scheme of ideas and as speculation—the latter characterized as a dangerous sense of the term. This distinction, however, should not be taken as absolute. Speculation or hypothesis can indeed provide the basis for developing theory as articulated conceptual knowledge. After all, the ideas that do get developed have to come from somewhere; they require a starting point, something to analyze and develop. Hunches, intuitions, feelings —"speculation" in the broad sense of the term—can provide just that. Descartes' dreaming visitation from the very Angel of Truth, providing the conceptual seed for much of his subsequent work, is but a dramatic example of a commonplace phenomenon.[13] It may be dangerous at best to think of ideas in their rudimentary state as theory in its own right, but the very notion of developing theory assumes a continuum from speculation to organized conceptual knowledge. Theory may result from the analysis of existing theory, and then again it may not. Its domain is the world of ideas, not just developed ideas.

Tied in with this developmental continuum is another missing element in Austin's argument: our varying degrees of awareness of concepts at different stages of their development toward conceptual knowledge. Consider the concept of archival description. Archivists have engaged in the practice of describing records since time out of mind, but only in recent years have they begun to articulate the concept of description—to hold it up to view and analyze it deliberately.[14] Considering the sometimes impressive descriptive work done in the past, archivists have obviously been employing some powerful ideas in this work—often, it would seem, of the methodological sort — even if they have only recently begun to explore their roots and implications in any depth. Though clearly not a barrier to successful work, this lack of awareness has precluded the development of descriptive theory, since analysis and development of concepts can only occur when ideas are held in mind. It is possible to know without knowing that one knows or to describe records successfully without special awareness of the conceptual underpinnings of that work. But only by bringing assumptions, intuitions, methods into the light can one begin the laborious path toward knowing that one knows by analyzing those prototheoretical roots and developing them conceptually. If this is true, it follows that the further development, organization, and testing of concepts along the path to full-fledged knowledge requires at least an equal awareness of those ideas.

If awareness of ideas is necessary for the development of conceptual knowledge, if ideas can exist in a state of development anywhere along a continuum from speculation to knowledge, and if methodology is a necessary intermediary between theory and practice, then it is reasonable to urge that archivists' ideas inevitably underlie their practice, whether they are aware of it or not. Austin's argument, if properly qualified, can stand. Archivists may not necessarily employ fully developed concepts in their work (although they may); they may not necessarily be aware of those ideas while working (although they may); and the ideas they do employ, whatever their degree of development or the level of awareness with which they are held, may have more of a methodological than a theoretical cast. This is not to say that *theory*, in the full meaning of the term, always underlies practice, but that ideas always do—and ideas are the stuff that theory is made of.

From this perspective, there is nothing radical about the claim that ideas always and inevitably underlie archival practice, whether archivists are aware of them or not. This holds true not only for the technical aspects of archival work but also for the managerial or administrative aspects of that work. According to one commentator, "every act of a manager rests on assumptions about what has happened and conjectures about what will happen; that is to say it rests on theory."[15] If this argument either strikes a responsive chord or grates on one's nerves, chances are that it is being viewed from one side or the other of the theory-practice distinction. However, if conjectures or speculations can be distinguished from theory as conceptual knowledge but seen to provide the basis for such theory, then there is little here to get excited about. The argument amounts to a claim that archival managers, like line archivists, have minds and, because they use their minds, what they do is evidence of what they believe. Those administrators who choose to analyze, develop, organize, and test the ideas that guide their work provide contributions to organizational theory and may even work from existing theory of this kind. But that is not the same as suggesting that assumptions and conjectures—the stuff of everyday activity for managers and professionals alike—can be equated with theory—especially not if theory is viewed as organized conceptual knowledge.

The same holds true for theorists as for archival managers. Inadvertently, perhaps, the tacit separation between thinking and doing in Austin's argument implies that theorists—or those who consciously examine ideas—are not doers in any real sense. There may be some truth to this, but it depends on what is meant by "doing." Theorizing itself can reasonably be considered a form of activity consisting of the practical application of certain ideas during the analysis of the concepts it happens to be focusing on—these underlying ideas being generally taken for granted as assumptions. It may be that, if developed, such ideas belong to theoretical fields outside the distinct sphere of archival thought, such as logic and epistemology. Still, while such working assumptions may not be specifically archival in nature, a double standard would be required to view archival theorists as somehow set apart from practitioners, even if their own practical activity does not necessarily have any immediate and obvious connection to the practical activity of clinicians in the same field. We may not all do the same kind of work all the time, but we all work — with ideas.

In all areas of archival endeavor —theoretical, managerial, technical, or professional— ideas inevitably underlie practice, however aware of them any of us may be at any given time. If developed, those ideas can contribute to theory, either directly within the field of archives or in related fields that archivists draw on for support.

THEORY AND SCHOLARSHIP

So far we have distinguished theory from the methodological and practical aspects of archival work. Viewing theory as conceptual knowledge also makes it possible to distinguish between theory and other kinds of archival knowledge. If it is reasonable to say that archivists have and use ideas, it is possible to add that archivists' use of their ideas results in knowledge.

As in the discussion of theory and practice, professional or technical archival work again provides the clearest example of what is meant. For instance, archivists not only maintain the order of documents originally provided by the creator because they have certain theoretical ideas about the nature of a fonds and a resulting methodology. They also gain knowledge about the particular body of records they are arranging. It is not simply that they hone their arranging skills by experience; they also gain a systematic understanding of what documents were made, received, and kept, how and why this was done, and how these activities changed or did not change over time. Accordingly, if scholarship can be seen as the examination of existing things in light of conceptions about reality and the best way of discovering it, then the note in an archival inventory describing the types of documents in question, their extent, and their relation to the creator clearly represents an example of archival scholarship. Perhaps there has been uneven recognition of such scholarship within the research community in general.[16] However, it has at least become increasingly recognized as such within the archival community itself. As argued by one commentator, archivists can reasonably be viewed as "researchers par excellence of institutions and the documents that they produce," to the extent that "institutional research from the perspective of archival science is one of the fundamental scientific tasks of the highest levels of the profession."[17]

This distinction between theory and scholarship marks off two broad areas of archival knowledge: the conceptual and the empirical. This is not to imply that an absolute division exists between the two or that they offer competing approaches to archival knowledge. There is no need to choose between the two or argue that one or the other provides the best approach to archival research, as one might be inclined to do if the distinction implied something akin to the often-presumed split between rationalism and empiricism. From the perspective of this study, theoretical or conceptual knowledge pertains to the examination of ideas as such, whereas scholarly or empirical knowledge pertains to examination of the particular facts in the archivist's world. An archivist as scholar may explore the nature of a particular fonds in his or her care and, as theorist, explore the nature of the fonds as a concept. Fuller development of these two general areas of research will together provide a full and rounded body of knowledge.

For the present purpose of illustrating the conceptual view of archival theory, there is no need to examine the relations between these two areas of knowledge in great detail, but it may be useful to point out the relation of dependence that exists between theory and scholarship. As mentioned above, empirical studies always presuppose concepts. These concepts need not be fully developed, but they must always exist in one form or another. This relation to theory applies in all areas of archival scholarship, not just those that result from or form an aspect of professional practice. Consider archival history or the history of archival ideas. This area of research can be clearly distinguished from archival theory and exemplifies the dependence of scholarship on theory. It is one thing to ask how ideas arose, developed, or spread; it is another thing to ask what those ideas mean and whether they are true. Describing the history of an idea or explaining its sociological roots is not the same thing as examining the logical structure of the idea itself. Nor can it serve as a substitute.[18] The question as to whether, or to what degree, Plato borrowed his theory of ideas or forms from the Pythagoreans merits attention, but does not go very far toward determining what he meant or whether he was right.

Perhaps an example may clarify this argument somewhat. It has been suggested that a body of archival theory will result from "recognizing patterns in the generation and management of archives in any legal and social reality and in any time."[19] In this view, a work like Posner's on ancient archives would be considered theoretical.[20] Still, without denying the value of such work or the need for more of it, one may wonder where these patterns come from and how we recognize them. Historiographers and philosophers have urged time and again that facts do not "speak for themselves."[21] Finding the relevant facts, recognizing meaningful patterns among them, and providing persuasive interpretations of both facts and patterns all depend on a priori conceptions. These conceptions are assumptions, ideas that guide the search for and recognition of patterns. They provide the light by which those patterns are seen.[22] Using the categories discussed earlier, these patterns and interpretations can be considered a form of archival knowledge falling within the category of scholarship rather than theory, because they result from the use of fundamental ideas.

Archival theory, from this standpoint, would result from an analysis of the basic concepts used in arriving at the patterns. Accordingly, Posner's book would properly be considered what he himself called it, an "essay in archival history"; in particular, an attempt to interpret the material before him in light of prior assumptions about the nature of archives.[23] He may have, in one sense, been testing the hypothesis that archives were the same then as now. But that hypothesis logically requires some previous assumption about the nature of archives; for example, that they are records made and received in the course of practical affairs. An examination of that assumption — an analysis of the idea itself, the assumption in light of which Posner saw the patterns that he did — would clearly be a contribution to archival theory, at least on the view that theory is conceptual knowledge resulting from the analysis of ideas. The use of that assumption in a different sort of investigation would contribute to archival scholarship — as Posner did so admirably.

NORMATIVE AND DESCRIPTIVE THEORY

The attempt to clarify the view of archival theory underlying this study has so far entailed distinguishing theory from methodology and practice, to place it within an overall view of archival work, and from scholarship, to place it more narrowly within the realm of archival knowledge. This view can be further clarified by examining the distinction made in the last chapter between two potential approaches to archival theory: the normative and the descriptive. Both forms of conceptual knowledge can be detected in common language and applied in general terms to archival usage. The normative or programmatic kind results from the analysis of ideas relating to the desirability of human action, whereas the descriptive or explanatory sort results from analyzing ideas relating to the nature of the world or human action. In broad archival terms, at least on the face of it, descriptive theory would accordingly aim at understanding and explaining the facts about what archivists and their clients do and the nature of the material they have to deal with. Normative theory, by contrast, would aim at clarifying and evaluating the ideas that guide archivists in all areas of their activity.

Before determining whether this distinction can be sustained beyond the heuristic uses made of it in the last chapter, further consideration of its nature is required. What exactly does this distinction between normative and explanatory theory amount to? In this regard, consider the two different senses in which the term *practice* is commonly used.[24] On one hand, it can refer without any evaluative overtones to what is in fact done. In this sense, it is the equivalent of "behavior" as a neutral term. Scholarly studies of persons who use archival repositories are generally seen as dealing with practice in this sense, as they explore who uses what, when, where, how, and why.[25] They may also go a step further and suggest policies that repositories ought to adopt, given the facts of user behavior that they have discovered. But advocacy of this sort, however justified, goes beyond the meaning of explaining behavior in the sense used here. Studies of the facts about how archivists describe records also deal with practice in this neutral sense. They may quite rightly go on to recommend particular descriptive methods and standards. However, in so doing, they too go beyond explanation of practice in this first sense.[26]

In contrast with this meaning, *practice* can also refer to appropriate action—what ought to be done, as opposed to what is in fact done. This is the meaning of the term intended when one speaks of professional practice in the context of archival education. In at-

tempting to equip students with the tools to accomplish successful
work, reference may be made to the diverse ways in which archivists actually perform various professional functions, such as arranging and describing records. But a disservice is done them and
their future employers if no attempt is made to evaluate those
various approaches with an eye toward what is in fact acceptable.
This normative sense of the term is also implied in the notion of
practice as what is typically or habitually done, as in "common
practice." Here there may not be quite the explicit forcefulness of
the normative sense, as in "professional practice," but the phrase
implies that "what is done here" is what ought to be done. It has
been done, is done, and will continue to be done, because it works
well enough. Since common practice and professional practice are
no doubt one and the same in most archival repositories, this
distinction is of no great moment. However, both uses of *practice*
do serve to illustrate the normative meaning of the term.

Descriptive or explanatory theory, as described, for instance, by
Burke, does not in any direct way concern itself with appropriate
action or proper professional practice. As nonevaluative as the
descriptive aspects of user studies or studies of existing arrangement or appraisal practices, it seeks to develop an overall conceptual framework explaining the facts of archival life. It takes those
facts as it finds them, analyzing the underlying concepts in an effort
to find the clearest and most precise possible explanation. Archival
knowledge, from this perspective, is knowledge of archival phenomena. As such, it may provide understanding, but it has no
answer to the actor's question about *why* things ought to be done
in a certain way or to what end. Normative theory, by contrast,
serves to answer exactly such questions. It does not always provide
answers to them immediately or directly, however, partly because
of the methodological translation required between theory and
practice. But this connection with practice and methodology ensures that its ultimate ability to answer such questions provides a
key to evaluating the worth of such theory.

If viewed abstractly, the normative and descriptive approaches
to archival theory can thus be distinguished from each other in very
broad outline. Could they conceivably provide complementary
paths toward a full range of conceptual knowledge, if developed
sufficiently? Though intellectually polite, in a pluralistically toler-
ant sense, this suggestion leaves unanswered the important ques-

tion of just how these two approaches to conceptual knowledge relate to each other. Even more, it provides no clue to determining how they fit together within the presumably larger whole of which they are both parts—archival theory. The distinction as it stands fails to accomplish this because it implies that description and evaluation must be separated from each other conceptually, as distinct kinds of theoretical activity. Archivists, it is implied, typically ask—or ought to ask—two sorts of theoretical question, one dealing with what is the case and the other with what ought to be done. For example, the question of how archivists appraise (or arrange or describe) records must be separated from the question of how they ought to appraise (or arrange or describe) them. The linkage between these questions, however, and a resulting view of the whole of archival theory, remains a mystery.

Less mysterious is the source of the snares set by the basic distinction between description and evaluation as potential approaches to archival theory. We are clearly dealing here with the old bugbear of fact and value, "is" versus "ought"—and the difficulty of bridging the two conceptually. It takes little effort to imagine, were some such distinction generally accepted in archival circles, theorists eventually setting up camps on either side of the divide, as if part of two cultures. On one side, objective archival scientists would be weighing and measuring data about phenomena in value-free neutrality. On the other, self-anointed archival preachers would be mouthing gnomic phrases or scorching sermons (a matter of temperament) about goodness, beauty, and the archival way of life. Between the two, the rest of us would be trying to get on with the same old job, thinking our own thoughts about such thinkers.

An attempt to save this distinction by linking description and evaluation could take a variety of forms. One way of avoiding their separation would be to subordinate descriptive to normative theory. In this view, certain relations would be judged to exist of necessity between the two, whatever their state of development, given the nature of archival work. Most important of these relations, it might be claimed, would be the inevitable primacy of the normative approach to theory.

The argument might run as follows. Normative theory is theory from the actor's perspective, its overall aim being to provide the best possible conceptual tools for accomplishing the job that archi-

vists are charged by their societies with doing. Because this practi-
cality of archival work is central to any reasonable characterization
of what archivists are about, the normative approach to theory
must take precedence over the descriptive. Given that archivists
exist to perform a social function, having a mission in the world—a
general theory, as Stielow calls it—description of phenomena cannot be an end in itself. It may be an end, but one instrumental to
achieving that overall mission. Yes, there are two distinct theoretical activities, but they follow a definite order: archivists first describe phenomena and then evaluate the implications of such
description for practice, all of this taking place within the framework of the overall mission. If, for example, archivists do in fact
appraise (or arrange or describe) records in a certain way, how
should they appraise (or arrange or describe) them? In other words,
archivists describe to evaluate, to attain their goals.

This view of the relation between the descriptive and the
normative approaches to theory has much to commend it. Most
importantly, it brings the notion of a general theory or mission into
the equation. This makes it possible to overcome the implied
dichotomy between "is" and "ought" that creeps into the concept
of description and evaluation as distinct but equal theoretical
activities. However, even while drawing the two together hierarchically, this view still conceives those activities as separable and
leaves the link between the two problematic. The method of moving from one activity to the other and thereby fitting them together
within the larger whole remains unclear.

Another possibility, the one adopted in this study, is to view the
normative and descriptive as two aspects of a unified approach to
theory. In this view, neither can exist without the other, both of
them comprising a single kind of theory and a single approach,
working conjointly like the blades of a scissors.[27] In any given
study, or even at different points within the same study, the emphasis may be more on one than on the other. But a single study
need not be a complete investigation which, in this view, requires
both description and evaluation. In examining the concept of public records, for example, the present work offers both a description
of how the various terms involved are used and an evaluation of
them. Some sections take on the appearance more of one than the
other. In terms of the whole investigation, however, this entails not
so much describing and then evaluating as rather doing both

toward the single end of arriving at the most workable concept.[28] What in fact brings the two together within a single approach is their subordination, not one to the other, but to this overall aim.

In speaking of an overall aim, I am of course referring to the goal of any particular conceptual investigation. But I also wish to suggest that the particular goals of specific studies are subordinate to the overall mission of the field of which they form a part. That, after all, is how one can tell whether a particular study has relevance to a given field and is indeed even part of it. Perception of this sort clearly depends on how a field defines itself. If, for example, historians view themselves as working together toward an understanding of the human past, then they would have reason to question the relevance of supposedly historical research into, say, attitudes toward the present government or the history of the Earth's crustal movements. If this is true in general, then it is reasonable to urge that, for archivists, all investigation is subordinate to Stielow's "mission statement" or "general theory," Cook's "philosophy," Haworth's "purpose"—to the fundamental enterprise of determining the overall nature, purpose, and meaning of archival endeavor.[29]

For archivists, this subordination of theory to mission not only provides a way of determining the relevance of any given investigation, assuming always that there is agreement on the nature of that mission.[30] It also draws together description and evaluation as two aspects of a single approach to theory by determining the structure of investigation. If, as I am assuming, the achievement of certain social goals is central to the archival mission—or if archivists are involved in an applied field—then the subordination of theory to mission implies that investigation, to be whole and complete, exists ultimately to further those goals. This does not mean that it necessarily concerns itself immediately or directly with solving practical problems or even with developing methods for solving them. As a conceptual enterprise, theory necessarily claims the time and distance needed to explore ideas and issues that may at first blush seem irrelevant to the press of daily work. However, because it exists as a component within the archival mission, a commitment to the practical work that archivists do in the world provides theory's starting point, its final end, and between these, its overall structure. Archivists describe *and* evaluate to attain their goals. Theory is indeed "only so good as it serves the work"—at least if "the work" is taken to include not just practice but the overall mission that theory, methodology, and practice all exist to further.[31] In other words, there is a teleological dimension to all investigation within the archival field.[32]

ARCHIVAL SCIENCE AND THE DISCIPLINE OF ARCHIVES

The discussion so far has distinguished several basic categories within the overall work that archivists do: philosophy or mission, theory, methodology, practice, and scholarship. By placing these categories within a general outline of the nature of archival work, the several parts of the preceding discussion can be conveniently brought together. As a whole, the three categories of theory, methodology, and practice constitute the part of archival work that I would call archival science. *Science* is a useful term, not because it implies anything grand, but because of its common division into two elements, pure and applied. "Pure" relates to the theoretical part of archival science, its basic ideas about the nature of things. "Applied," by contrast, relates to the practical and methodological components, both of which comprise archivists' use of their basic ideas. Wherever one might place archives within a hierarchy of sciences, the simple fact that it can be usefully characterized as a theoretical, methodological, and practical endeavor warrants its inclusion within this sphere.

On reflection, however, it becomes clear that there is more to archival work than archival science. As pointed out earlier, archival practice often results in products with a significant scholarly component. Because of this scholarly element, archives may be considered a discipline as well as a profession. *Discipline,* as commonly used, denotes a form of study with a distinct methodology used to gain knowledge. A discipline encompasses both a way of gaining knowledge—rules of procedure that discipline the scholar's search—and the resulting knowledge itself. Archives, therefore, may reasonably be considered a discipline, in that its methodology provides a way of gaining knowledge through the practical application of concepts. However, the relation between archival methodology and scholarship differs from the relation between the two in other disciplines without a practical, professional dimension. What distinguishes the archival discipline is the connection between its methodology and the theoretical ideas discussed earlier.

Archival methodology derives from archival theory, while archival practice and scholarship are two products of the application of that methodology. This relationship between theory, methodology, and scholarship implies that archival methodology helps archival scholars gain knowledge according to theoretical ideas about the nature of the same aspect of reality that they are trying to understand. Theoretical ideas about the nature of a fonds, for example— generally or in the abstract—dictate the archival methodology by which a particular fonds is examined by the archivist, which in turn determines the resulting scholarly product.

Other disciplines do not always have such a connection between theory and methodology. History, for example, has its own methodology and body of scholarship, but historians do not generally consider it part of their legitimate concern to discuss or profess ideas about the nature of human history as such. While theories of the nature of history have been set forth over the years, they do not usually find a place of primary importance in discussions about historical methodology.[33] Accordingly, one may say that if history is a discipline, archives is both a science and a discipline at the same time. Like history, it seeks knowledge, but it also has immediate practical tasks to accomplish and an integral theoretical component.

Although archival scholarship often results from the practical application of concepts, it also results in many cases from empirical research that does not have this direct connection between theory, methodology, and practice. A study of the way clients use archival resources does not have the same direct connection to theory and methodology as do certain parts of an inventory or appraisal report. The same would apply to all empirical studies that examine the processes and results of archival practice—studies that are about such phenomena, as opposed to scholarship that is part of that practice itself. Nonetheless, few would deny that such research is both scholarly and of great importance to archivists. If so, then a place must be found for such scholarship within the overall characterization of archival endeavor.

Considering the distinction made above between archival science and the discipline of archives, research of this sort can reasonably be considered part of the archival discipline, which comprises the whole range of archival knowledge. A main difference between this sort of scholarship and the sort that results from the direct application of archival concepts will in many cases be the discipline from which it adopts its methodology. User studies, for instance, may well borrow proven methods from the social sciences, while studies such as Posner's on ancient archives reasonably draw on the discipline of history. In all such cases, though, it is worth keeping in mind that the phenomena under examination bear the imprint of archival concepts, simply because they result from archival practice, which derives from archival theory and methodology. This is not a liability, even if the concepts which such research must assume for the sake of investigation are of necessity open to the analytical scrutiny of archival theory. On the contrary, a great strength of such studies lies in their ability to enrich the archival discipline by providing a view from outside archival science. It follows from the discussion of the descriptive and normative approaches to theory that such studies may potentially contribute to archival theory through development of its inductive component, which may in turn lead toward enhancements in methodology and new forms of practice. In other words, scholarship of this sort, while beginning outside archival science proper, has the potential to become a part of that science.

Although it is not my purpose here to develop anything like a complete model of archival endeavor, the foregoing discussion of scholarship within the discipline of archives invites brief mention of its interdisciplinary character. Archivists may have their own science and discipline, but in various areas of activity they draw on knowledge developed in other fields. The variety of such knowledge inevitably changes to some extent over time, for archivists necessarily redefine what is useful to them in relation to their own changing priorities. Library science, for example, has in recent times provided fruitful analogies and strategies toward the development of standards for archival description, while information science has suggested tools for structuring archival access systems in automated form.[34] Other fields can provide consistent contributions to archival work over time. Diplomatics, for instance—"the study of the genesis, inner constitution, forms, natural aggregation, and transmission of archival documents"—helps archivists determine the relations between documentary "context, content, and form."[35] Organization theory, management science, and public administration offer nourishment for those aspects of archival work with a managerial dimension.[36] Similarly, the field of law provides elements essential to successful administration of access and acquisition, to name only two activities, while contributing concepts useful for determining the legal value that records may possess.[37]

As these examples suggest, knowledge and methods from other areas can relate to archival work in a number of different ways, presenting a complex mosaic of interdisciplinarity. As used by archivists, they can be auxiliary or supplementary, ancillary or subordinate, analogical or suggestive, all the while retaining their integrity as separate fields.[38] Some of them may even have more than a single kind of relation to the archival field, given their own inherent complexities.

Consider, in this regard, archivists' various uses of history. An understanding of the history of records making and keeping undoubtedly contributes to the archivist's ongoing education, which suggests that historical scholarship of this kind may be considered part of the discipline of archives. Historical works such as Posner's on ancient archives can also spur reflection on theoretical questions and perhaps even provide a testing ground for some aspects of theory. In addition, there is a certain historical sensibility that archivists habitually bring to bear on various aspects of their work. While arranging a fonds, for instance, writing an inventory, or appraising a series of records, the archivist must take due notice of the social, cultural, legal, political, and administrative environment in which the documents were made and kept. Because the records involved were created over time, there is of necessity a historical dimension to the analysis required in such work. In cases of this sort, it can be argued that aspects of historical sensibility, if not method or content, have rightly been drawn into archival science and absorbed as parts of its methodology. History can also be seen to relate to archival work in those instances where historical method serves as a mode of theoretical inquiry. Works such as Berner's *Archival Theory and Practice in the United States*, for example, may be considered works of archival history from one perspective. Looked at in another way, however, they can reasonably be construed as theoretical studies of archival concepts and functions articulated within a rhetorical framework based on historical narrative. Such works suffer little from being viewed either way.[39]

To thus distinguish several of the relations between archival endeavor and the discipline of history by no means implies that the

two should or need be divorced. The very concept of interdisciplinarity implies connections, the question being one of determining
exactly what those connections are. To distinguish is not to divorce
but rather to classify, categorize, arrange intellectually for the sake
of clarity and understanding. For example, only a rash person
would conclude, from the conceptually useful distinction between
mind and body, that actual human lives can therefore be separated
into two kinds of substance or material. A core of archival knowledge can likewise be distinguished from the knowledge and out-
look of disciplines such as history, on which archival work may
draw. This in no way denies the possibility—indeed, the inevita-
bility—of mutual interplay and nourishment between them.[40]

This brief look at the interdisciplinary character of archival work
has attempted only to suggest some of the complexities involved
and how their configuration can change over time. What binds the
whole together in any period is archivists' working definition of
themselves, their role, and its meaning. In order to be as clear as
possible on this point, some clarification of terminology will be
useful. A number of terms have been suggested for this constella-
tion of ideas: *philosophy, purpose, general theory, mission.* All of them
have merit, but none quite covers the ground I have in mind.
Purpose and *mission* are too narrow, since a group's purpose derives
from its nature and its mission derives from particularizing the
ends embodied in that overall purpose. In other words, if one asks
where archivists' purpose comes from or why this purpose rather
than that one, a reasonable answer would tend to refer back to the
prior question of identity. To answer a similar question about the
archival mission would refer back to the question of purpose.
General theory and *philosophy* are more comprehensive terms, since
both could embody the concepts of purpose, mission, and identity.
General theory, however, has two difficulties. The term has its own
history in the social sciences, as Stielow reminds us, and it seems
best to characterize archival issues in strictly archival terms. On the
other hand, potential confusion resides in its employment of the
term *theory,* which has already been used here in the specific sense
of conceptual knowledge, and I by no means wish to imply that
these overall ideas about identity, purpose, and meaning can be
reduced to questions of metatheory or the theory of theory, as if the
whole thing were a matter of epistemology alone.[41] *Philosophy* in a
very general sense comes closest to encompassing these ideas,

although its tendency to imply something grand but vague makes it less than ideal, let alone its more specific use as the name of an academic discipline that has at times tended to divorce itself from the very sorts of question at issue.[42] My own preference—less grand, almost as vague, but not directly associated with any discipline or disciplines, implying answers to logically prior questions, or employing terms used elsewhere in the discussion so far—is for the term *worldview*. As used here, this term refers simply to an overall view of the world, to a concept or set of concepts about the nature of the archival world in particular, of the whole of things archival, and how it relates to the larger world of which it is a part.

In saying that archivists' worldview determines the configuration of interdisciplinarity in any given period, I am suggesting that answers to the broad questions of identity, meaning, and purpose provide a general sense of what is fitting, of what kinds of interdisciplinarity are acceptable and what kinds are not. As with archival theory, such concepts need not be articulated or developed to be pervasive or powerful. They may work upon us, for good or ill, as parts of the assumptive world that guides our overall patterns of thought, our sense of what is reasonable and right. In this view of things, more is involved here than archivists' sense of what disciplines appropriately touch the boundaries of their world and in what way. The implication is that the whole of archival endeavor takes its shape from archivists' answers to the questions comprising their worldview. Archival science, the discipline of archives, and the place of theory within the two; professional ethics, with its own methodology and practice perhaps, paralleling or mirroring archival science; and the professional culture of the archivist, combining elements of shared history, vision, responsibility, language, and purpose—all the various aspects of archival work and thinking, however one may construe them, exist from this perspective as manifestations of the archival worldview. Evidence exists that the tools of theory can be successfully applied to the conceptual aspects of archivists' worldview and may well play a significant role in its clarification and development in the years ahead.[43] Theory in the sense of conceptual knowledge, however, is but one element of the whole.

This brief look at the nature of archival endeavor—"archival studies," from the academic point of view—can be summarized as follows. Within an overall worldview, archival studies consists of two overlapping and interdependent parts, which have here been called archival science and the discipline of archives.[44] The science is both pure and applied. The pure aspect relates to theory, understood here as the product of analyzing ideas about the fundamental entities in the archivist's world—archives, records, fonds, and so on. The applied aspect relates both to the methodological ideas derived from theory and to the practical application of those ideas. The discipline, on the other hand, comprises theory, methodology, and scholarship. In part, the methodology derives directly from the theory shared in common with archival science, in which case the scholarship results from an application of those basic ideas and results in knowledge of archives. For some purposes, however, the methodology incorporates or borrows methods from other disciplines, in which case the scholarship results from the filtering of theoretical ideas through these borrowed or adapted methods and results in knowledge about archives.

These categories within archival endeavor as a study, set down graphically in Figure 1, take on a slightly different configuration when looked at from the viewpoint of the content of that study, as set down in Figure 2. This content has to some extent been only implicit in the foregoing discussion. However, one may say that archival studies can be divided, not just into the categories of science and discipline, but also into the categories of knowledge and practice. Archival knowledge comprises both theory and scholarship, while archival practice consists of the great variety of activities resulting from the application of concepts—from the technical or professional work performed on, or on behalf of, the documents in archivists' care to the overall management of archival repositories. Methodology, from both points of view, remains an intermediate category, linking theory to practice and scholarship. In helping to distinguish archival science from the discipline of archives and archival knowledge from archival practice, the notion of theory as conceptual knowledge resulting from the analysis of ideas thus contributes to and finds its place within an overall understanding of the structure and content of archival endeavor.[45]

THE USES OF THEORY

Without making any great claims about the value of theory in archival work, one may still hold that it has its own role to play, as

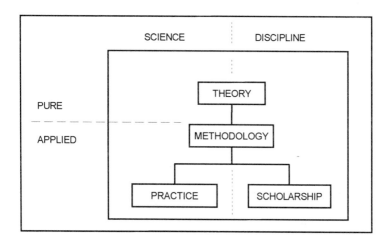

Figure 1. The Structure of Archival Studies

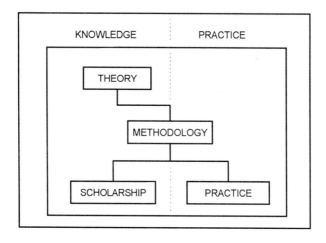

Figure 2. The Content of Archival Studies

do all the other components. Although indications of what I see that role as consisting of are implicit throughout this chapter, perhaps brief mention of the more salient ones will help round out the overall discussion. In general terms, the view of theory presented here can contribute to the development of archival endeavor because of the very fact that it focuses archivists' attention, and implicitly encourages concentrating at least some of their efforts, on theory—that is, on the analysis of concepts underlying all aspects of their work. In this view, ideas come first; they guide both practice and scholarship.

In thus focusing attention and concentrating effort on the analysis of ideas, this view of theory can contribute to the development of archival work in several areas. For one thing, the interdisciplinary character of archival studies requires the clarity of thought that the analysis of ideas can bring. When borrowing ideas developed in other areas of study and adapting them to their own needs, archivists have to be clear about the nature of those ideas and the implications of adapting them, in order to keep control of the intellectual direction in which they subsequently travel. Examination of concepts can also help to order the complexity of a field in which action results from the practical application of general ideas by means of a distinctive methodology. More particularly, clarification and development of those ideas provides a foundation for rationally structuring, and a continual means of evaluating, the overall approach to daily activity and its results. So, too, for archival education, since the view taken of the structure of the field bears as much on curriculum development as does the content available for teaching and the perceived relations with other disciplines and between theory, methodology, and practice—to all of which theory can contribute in various ways.[46] In addition, the influence of archivists' intellectual environment requires the clarity born of analysis, since all their ideas, whether adapted from other fields or not, are influenced by a host of cultural, legal, and political ideas forming part of the environment in which they think. Such ideas filter into all levels and almost all aspects of archival work, whether it be the formation of a worldview, the development of theory, or the management of a repository. A self-conscious analysis of ideas may not provide all the answers, but can make it possible to discover some of the ways in which archivists have unwittingly allowed that environment to shape their ideas, and then allow them to judge whether that "shape" is truly fitting. Analysis itself, or the habits of mind that it may engender, can also guard against easy acceptance of habitual or supposedly self-evident notions, while at the same time opening up and clarifying alternative views of the various elements of archival studies.[47] In exploring alternative views, archivists can discover new possibilities, different potential directions in which they might travel. Through finding out what their work could be, archivists will be better equipped to choose the best path to follow in the future.

All this is not to suggest that theory is a panacea of some sort or that it holds a privileged place in archival work. Its very strengths harbor potential liabilities such as overabstraction and inappropriate prescription, if detached from its subordinate place within the whole. Far from glamorous, theory consists mainly of conceptual spadework. It may be useful, but no more useful than all the other forms of work that contribute to the archival endeavor. Like all spadework, theory exists for ends beyond itself.

NOTES

1. The focus of the present discussion precludes a detailed examination of the relations between words and things. However, it may be said that the Socratic reference is intended to suggest that nothing in this study rests on any distinction between definitions of words and analyses of ideas. For present purposes, a real definition is the verbal reflection of a concept, a proposition about the nature of things (Morris R. Cohen and Ernest Nagel, *An Introduction to Logic and Scientific Method* [New York: Harcourt, Brace & Co., 1934], p. 230). The reader need not worry overmuch about occasional shifts between what look like definitions and analyses.

It should be evident, but may nonetheless be stated explicitly at the outset, that in this study the terms *idea, concept, notion,* and *view* can be considered synonyms except where the context dictates otherwise.

2. Logically, the analysis of *all* archival concepts can be considered theoretical in this sense, whether the ideas are simple or complex, commonplace or exotic, central or peripheral. What must be taken into account in any given instance of analysis is the position of the concept in question within the overall scheme of archival ideas and its relation to more general, more specific, and parallel ideas. For clarity's sake, however, the present discussion will be limited to basic or general concepts.

3. For an example of the linguistic, if not conceptual, confusion that can result from this usage, see Chapter 1.

4. Burke, "The Future Course of Archival Theory," p. 45.

5. See Mary Sue Stephenson, "Deciding Not to Build the Wall: Research and the Archival Profession," *Archivaria* 32 (Summer 1991): 145-51.

6. These comments simply describe how the distinction between theory and practice looks through the lens of the analysis-of-ideas view of archival theory. A more formal treatment would first require demonstrating how this view of theory can actually generate those categories. It might be noted, though, that if one starts from the assumption that theory deals purely with ideas and that ideas can be analyzed in their own right, then it follows that ideas can be distinguished from their application.

7. Hilary Jenkinson, "The English Archivist: A New Profession," in his *Selected Writings of Sir Hilary Jenkinson*, edited by Roger H. Ellis and Peter Walne (Gloucester: Alan Sutton, 1980), p. 237.

8. Giorgio Cencetti, "Il fondamento teorico della dottrina archivistica," *Archivi* VI (1939): 8; reprinted in his *Scritti Archivistici* (Roma: Il Centro di Ricerca Editore, 1970), p. 39.

9. For a more detailed exploration of these issues, see Terry Eastwood, ed., *The Archival Fonds: From Theory to Practice* (Ottawa: Bureau of Canadian Archivists, Planning Committee on Descriptive Standards, 1992).

10. John Austin, *Lectures on Jurisprudence or the Philosophy of Positive Law*, (London: John Murray, 1885), p. 116. An elaboration of this argument can be found in Immanuel Kant, *On the Old Saw: That May Be Right in Theory But It Won't Work in Practice*, trans. E. B. Ashton (Philadelphia: University of Pennsylvania Press, 1974), pp. 41-43.

11. As quoted by Terry Eastwood in his "Unity and Diversity in the Development of Archival Science in North America" (speech delivered on the occasion of the 25th anniversary of the Special School for Archivists and Librarians at the University of Rome, September 1989), p. 1.

12. The term *instrumentalize* is borrowed from Terry Eastwood, letter to the author, March 21, 1991.

13. See, for example, Theodore Roszak, *The Cult of Information: The Folklore of Computers and the True Art of Thinking* (New York: Pantheon Books, 1986), pp. 210-20. Reference to extensive research in this area can be found in "The Making of Hypotheses," *MANAS* 2 (July 27, 1949): 6-7.

14. See Luciana Duranti, "Origin and Development of the Concept of Archival Description," *Archivaria* 35 (Spring 1993): 47-54.

15. D. S. Pugh, ed., *Organization Theory: Selected Readings*, 2nd ed. (Harmondsworth, England: Penguin Books, 1984), p. 9.

16. Ann E. Pederson, "Writing and Research," paper prepared for the XIIth International Congress on Archives, Montreal, September 1992, p. 20. The scholarly quality of the archival note in an inventory is remarked on in passing by David B. Gracy et al. in *Inventories and Registers: A Handbook of Techniques and Examples* (Chicago: Society of American Archivists, 1976), p. 21.

17. Pedro López, "Archival Training: Specialists and/or Generalists," paper prepared for the XIIth International Congress on Archives, Montreal, September 1992, p. 9. See also Richard J. Cox and Helen W. Samuels, "The Archivist's First Responsibility: A Research Agenda to Improve the Identification and Retention of Records of Enduring Value," *American Archivist* 51 (Winter and Spring 1988): 30.

18. Cohen and Nagel, *An Introduction to Logic,* pp. 389-90.

19. Terry Eastwood, "Nurturing Archival Education in the University," *American Archivist* 51 (Summer 1988): 235 and note 29 at the same place. In fairness, it should be pointed out that Eastwood is working, in this context, from a twofold division of archival studies into the basic categories of theory and practice. As a result, his use of the word *theory* involves the whole of what has in the foregoing discussion been called archival knowledge — which, in turn, has been divided into the categories of theory and scholarship. Judging from the definitions of theory given in an earlier draft of this article — "extended *definition* of the nature of things" (edited to read "extended *exploration*" in the published version, p. 234) — there is no reason to imagine any necessary disagreement, finally, between his argument and the one presented here (Terry Eastwood, "Nurturing Archival Studies In A Canadian University: A Personal View," June 1988, p. 8, emphasis added).

20. Ernst Posner, *Archives in the Ancient World* (Cambridge, MA: Harvard University Press, 1972).

21. "How odd it is," thought Darwin, "that anyone should not see that all observation must be for or against some view, if it is to be of any service" (cited in Cohen and Nagel, *An Introduction to Logic,* p. 197).

22. As the Greeks used to ask: if you do not know what something is, how can you try to discover it, and how will you know when you have found it, even if you do so (Plato, *Meno* 80d, in *Plato: The Collected Dialogues,* ed. Edith Hamilton and Huntington Cairns [Princeton, NJ: Princeton University Press, Bollingen Series 71, 1961], p. 363) See also Henry Steele Commager, *The Nature and Study of History* (Columbus, OH: Charles K. Merrill, 1965), p. 5; and Morris R. Cohen, *Reason and Nature: The Meaning of Scientific Method,* 2nd ed. (New York: Macmillan, Free Press of Glencoe, 1964), pp. 76-82.

23. Posner, *Archives in the Ancient World,* p. vii, emphasis added.

24. See Williams, *Keywords,* pp. 267-68.

25. See, for example, the examples of suggested studies into the use of archives in Lawrence Dowler, "The Role of Use in Defining Archival Practice and Principles: A Research Agenda for the Availability and Use of Records," *American Archivist* 51 (Winter and Spring 1988): 74-86.

26. See, for instance, Bureau of Canadian Archivists, *Toward Descriptive Standards: Report and Recommendations of the Canadian Working Group on*

Archival Descriptive Standards (Ottawa: Bureau of Canadian Archivists, 1985).

27. The scissors image is borrowed from Morris R. Cohen's discussion of the principle of polarity in *A Preface to Logic* (Cleveland: World Publishing Company, Meridian Books, 1956), p. 88.

28. This may not be the best possible example, if only because, for reasons mentioned elsewhere, the descriptive aspect of the study deals mostly with existing definitions of the terms involved rather than attempting to develop a theoretical model inductively from the myriad examples that the definitions attempt to encompass. A study of this latter sort, though an incomplete investigation in itself, would provide a supplement to the present study and thereby enhance the example. But it would not alter the structural relation outlined here between its descriptive and evaluative components.

29. Stielow, "Archival Theory Redux and Redeemed," p. 23; Cook, "ACA Conference Overview," p. 3; Haworth, "The Principles Speak for Themselves," passim.

30. This is, of course, a large assumption, as archivists continue to work toward common and well reasoned answers to the questions of identity and purpose — the professional equivalent of what Ortega referred to more generally as the "last dramatic questions" (quoted from his *Toward a Philosophy of History* in "The Last Dramatic Questions," *MANAS* 29 [March 31, 1976]: 8).

31. Terry Eastwood, "Towards a Social Theory of Appraisal," in Craig, ed., *The Archival Imagination*, p. 72.

32. Some such assumption, which I am claiming is implicit in all archival investigation because of the nature of archival endeavor, often becomes explicit in archivists' formulation of research agendas, since the latter consciously attempt to direct research toward specific professional goals. The notion of an agenda presupposes answers of some sort to the larger questions of purpose and identity. See, for example, the group of articles introduced by Charles G. Palm, "Introduction to Archival Research Agendas," *American Archivist* 51 (Winter and Spring 1988): 24-27.

33. Jacques Barzun and Henry F. Graff, *The Modern Researcher*, 3rd ed. (New York: Harcourt Brace Jovanovich, 1977), pp. 157-65.

34. See, for example, Bureau of Canadian Archivists, Planning Committee on Descriptive Standards, *Rules for Archival Description* (Ottawa: Bureau of Canadian Archivists, 1990), pp. xi-xvii; and Bureau of Canadian Archivists, Planning Committee on Descriptive Standards, *Subject Indexing for Archives: Report of the Subject Indexing Working Group* (Ottawa: Bureau of Canadian Archivists, 1992). A useful annotated bibliography pertaining to automation in archives will be found in Marion Matters, ed., *Automated Records and Techniques in Archives: A Resource Directory* (Chicago: Society of American Archivists, 1990), pp. 12-37.

35. Society of American Archivists' draft *Guidelines for the Development of a Curriculum for a Master of Archival Studies* (Chicago: Society of American Archivists, 1993), p. 12, note 11.

36. A wide-ranging distillation of such scholarship can be found in Thomas Wilsted and William Nolte, *Managing Archival and Manuscript Repositories* (Chicago: Society of American Archivists, Archival Fundamentals Series, 1991).

37. See, for instance, Peterson and Peterson, *Archives and Manuscripts: Law*, passim. An extended discussion of the variety of studies that merit attention from archivists will be found in Eastwood, "Nurturing Archival Education," pp. 246-50.

38. Needless to say, these three categories by no means exhaust the possibilities. For a brief discussion of several kinds of interdisciplinarity, see the Society of American Archivists' draft *Guidelines for the Development of a Curriculum for a Master of Archival Studies*, p. 11, note 4. On the interdisciplinary character of archival work in general, see Luciana Duranti, "Comments on Hugh Taylor's and Tom Nesmith's Papers" (paper presented at the 13th Annual Conference of the Association of Canadian Archivists, Windsor, Ontario, June 8, 1988), p. 10.

39. Richard Berner, *Archival Theory and Practice in the United States: A Historical Analysis* (Seattle: University of Washington Press, 1983). See also, Luciana Duranti, "The Odyssey of Records Managers," *Records Management Quarterly* 23 (July 1989): 3-11, and (October 1989): 3-11. It has been pointed out that the more developed an area of study, the less it relies on history — at least in disciplines such as mathematics, physics, and biology; see Cohen, *Reason and Nature*, p. 370. The foregoing discussion, however, suggests that archival work as a whole will always have a significant historical component, although archival theory may well be found mixed with archival history less often as it develops analytically.

40. As discussed in the last chapter, and in contrast to the perspective offered here, the long association between archivists and historians has led some commentators to conclude that archival theory, as they characterize it, is best understood as a species of historiography. For example, see Burke, "The Future Course of Archival Theory," pp. 42-43, 45-46; and Roberts, "Archival Theory: Much Ado," pp. 69-72. A recent discussion of the issues involved can be found in Terry Eastwood, "Nailing a Little Jelly to the Wall of Archival Studies," *Archivaria* 35 (Spring 1993): 232-52.

41. By a seeming paradox, however, archival theory can provide one of the most useful approaches to these larger issues because, as Liv Mykland puts it, "Archives alone give archivists the *basis* of their identity. From them, archivists acquire their sense of worth and form ideas about the nature of their duties and their place in society" (Liv Mykland, "Protection and Integrity: The Archivist's Identity and Professionalism" [paper pre-

pared for the XIIth International Congress on Archives, Montreal, September 1992]: 2, emphasis added).

42. See, for example, Kenneth R. Seeskin, "Never Speculate, Never Explain: The State of Contemporary Philosophy," *American Scholar* 49 (Winter 1979-80): 19-33.

43. See, for example, Jane Parkinson, "Accountability in Archival Science," Master of Archival Studies thesis, University of British Columbia, 1993.

44. Though mentioned in passing, the place of ethics within the whole of archival work is ignored in this summary, not because I think it unimportant, but precisely because its very importance and the complex relations between it and the epistemological dimension of archival endeavor discussed here warrant more detailed treatment.

45. Although not within the compass of the present study, an extended treatment of the nature of archival theory as it relates to the structure and content of archival studies might usefully incorporate an examination of recent curricular developments in this field, to see what sorts of assumptions archival educators have in fact been applying when engaged in their own practical work of devising programs and courses. Examples of such developments can be found in the Association of Canadian Archivists, Education Committee, "Guidelines for the Development of a Two-Year Curriculum for a Master of Archival Studies Programme [December 1988]," Archivaria 29 (Winter 1989-90): 128-41; and the Society of American Archivists' draft *Guidelines for the Development of a Curriculum for a Master of Archival Studies*, passim.

46. This is not in the least to suggest that archival *education* should involve only theory. Quite obviously, the education of those involved in an applied field will fail unless it finds some way of combining theory and practice. Nonetheless, the view of archival theory espoused in this study does imply that ideas come first, as education comes before training.

47. For a discussion of the differences between the psychological feeling of certainty and logical demonstration, see Cohen, *Reason and Nature,* pp. 83-88.

Chapter 3

Records

RECORDS IN COMMON LANGUAGE AND LEGAL USAGE

The word *record* entered the English language during the Middle Ages. Filtered through French, it derives ultimately from the Latin word *recordari*, meaning "to remember, bring back to mind." This verb combines *re*, as in "again, back," with *cor, cordis*, which means "heart" or "mind" ("ari" signaling the infinitive mood). Like the Romans, we find it easy to remember things learned by heart. *Recordari* gave birth to the French "recorder," meaning "to remember for oneself, to recall to another," which led to the French noun *record* or "memory, a memory." The verb *recorder* became "recorden" in English, giving way eventually to "record," while the French noun "record" retained the same form and meaning in English.[1]

These early meanings of *record* in English, transferred from Latin and French, do not exhaust the field. They point rather to a general sense of the word, a core idea around which various meanings cluster. The noun, for instance, could refer to memory, a memory, or an account of something, while the verb could mean to remember, to memorize, to set down, to relate, to be mindful of, and several other things. Most of these senses of the word are obsolete, though it can be argued that those still in common use continue to reflect the root sense of the word: recollection.[2]

Among the meanings of *record* common to both medieval and modern times, two strains exist. These might be called the legal and literary uses of the word, from the kinds of examples cited in the *OED*. On the legal side, a standard definition might run as follows: "an authentic or official report of the proceedings in any cause coming before a court of record, together with the judgements given thereon, entered upon the rolls of court and affording indisputable evidence of the matter in question."[3] The corresponding literary definition would then be "an account of some fact or event preserved in writing or other permanent form; a document, monument, etc., on which such an account is inscribed."[4] As can be seen, though the literary or common meaning is somewhat broader, the two are related by the common idea of setting something down in writing for later recall.

It was not always so. Until the early thirteenth century, legal records were not written but oral. Summonses were issued by word of mouth, pleadings in court had to be spoken, and the memory of respected elders was considered proof of what had occurred. In fact, "to record" in the twelfth century meant essentially "to bear witness orally."[5] During the transition from oral to written records, judges apparently had to work largely from their memory of precedents and personal experience, relying on the written records mainly as a check.[6] These notions are partly brought together in the idea that

> Records be nothing else but memorials (or monuments) of things done before judges that have credit in that behalf...thus record (or testimony) is first contained within the breast of the Judge (as our law speaketh) and afterwards commited [sic] to the rolls, which are therefore figuratively speaking called Records also.[7]

Lack of evidence makes it difficult to determine if the literary or common meaning of the word also underwent a similar shift as writing came to predominate over memory. However, by the fourteenth and fifteenth centuries both the specialized legal and common meanings of *record* were the same as those in use today, as noted above in citations culled from the *OED*.[8]

INFORMATION, DOCUMENTS, AND RECORDS

In considering the two main definitions of *records* common among archivists today, most of this etymological material stands largely as contextual backdrop. Present purposes require scant discussion of the legal meaning of the term, and the distinction between oral and written records need not concern twentieth-century archivists overmuch, for it is largely a cultural matter whether something set down for later recall is recorded in oral or written form.[9] Still, the common meaning of *record* over the past six centuries or so has much in common with one of the two main archival definitions of the word today: "recorded information."[10]

Without pretending to a comprehensive terminological analysis, the present discussion will move forward with greater clarity and precision if this definition of records as recorded information is placed briefly within a rudimentary logical hierarchy of terms.[11] It might be noted, first of all, that "information" is the fundamental term from which the authors of the definition have decided, deliberately or not, to work. Information is the genus, and records are the species. If pressed back further, the hierarchy would include an even more fundamental genus of which information is a species—and so on, until some basic genus were reached, from which all the others ultimately derive. For the purposes of these authors, though, information (left undefined) is considered the basic category.

As well, it is evident that the species of information called records is differentiated from all other possible species of information by being "recorded." This differentiating attribute is the adjective that qualifies the noun, which in turn represents the particular species of the genus in question. Accordingly, as one can define man as the "featherless biped"—with "biped" being the genus and "featherless" the differentiating attribute of this particular species of biped, man—so one can say that the species "records" looks up the logical hierarchy to its genus, "information," and may be distinguished from all other species of information because it alone is qualified by the adjective "recorded."[12]

It will prove useful to further characterize these two elements of definition—the genus-species relationship and the differentiating attribute of the species—in slightly different terms. In particular, the distinction between these two elements of any workable definition can also be viewed as the difference between necessary and sufficient conditions. For example, *records,* as indicated, can be defined as "recorded information." In this case, before any given thing can be included within the category of records, it must first be part of the category of "information." If it does not fit within this category, it cannot possibly be considered a record. However, there may be any number of things one might call information that one would want to exclude from the category of records. Hence it may be said that while a given thing must necessarily fall within the bounds of "information" to be considered a record, only those kinds of information that are in fact recorded have all the qualities *sufficient* to qualify them as records proper.[13]

In a formal or technical sense, the definition of records as "recorded information" is sound. Unfortunately, it does not actually reveal much about what records are, because "information" is such a fuzzy word. While rising enormously in status over the last forty years, the term has perhaps decreased proportionately in clarity and precision—so much so that one respected commentator has seen fit to dub the term "an all-purpose weasel-word."[14]

Given the vagueness and ambiguity surrounding the word *information*, a strategic retreat to a classic definition may prove useful. For present purposes, there seems little reason for rejecting Samuel Johnson's terse definition of information: "intelligence given."[15] Both terms of the definition are useful. *Intelligence* refers to a message, something that makes sense—not gibberish, but something with an intellectual form capable of being shared by others. Intelligence "given" is intelligence conveyed or communicated— not necessarily with conscious intent, but nonetheless shared. Both telephone conversations and shards unearthed in archeological digs provide information.

When "intelligence given" is recorded, however, we encounter a message set down in more or less permanent form. Conscious intent to convey a message is evident in the act of recording, though not necessarily an intent to bridge time. Still, the message, while not necessarily being set down for later recall—to bridge time— nonetheless does so. There is a difference, for example, between simply writing a letter and deliberately making a carbon copy of it; the letter only inadvertently bridges time, if kept by the recipient and reread at a later date. Dr. Johnson's definition is thus of service to archivists in that it leads them toward a definition of records that provides some measure of objectivity. They may look at the material before them on its own account, not worrying about the original intentions of those who actually made or received it—while at the same time having the advantage of working from a sense of what those intentions *may* have been. This result of so defining records stems from the definition's proximity to the definition of *document* employed in diplomatics, which speaks of "the expression of ideas in a form which is both objectified (documentary) and syntactic (governed by rules of arrangement)."[16] Since North American archivists have for some time defined documents as synonymous with records in the sense of "recorded information," the term *documents* will henceforth be used when referring to records in this first sense. As well as following customary usage, this equation of documents and recorded information provides a measure of clarity, for it clears the path toward a single definition of records and a correspondingly more precise hierarchy of terms.[17]

RECORDS AND ARCHIVES

The second definition of *records* common to archivists today was set down by Theodore Schellenberg.

> All books, papers, maps, photographs, or other documentary materials, regardless of physical form or characteristics, made or received by any public or private institution in pursuance of its legal obligations or in connection with the transaction of its proper business and preserved or appropriate for preservation by that institution or its legitimate successor as evidence of its functions, policies, decisions, procedures, operations, or other activities or because of the informational value of the data contained therein.[18]

This definition can be analyzed more conveniently if its elements are set out in point form.

1. All books, papers, maps, photographs, or other documentary materials,
2. regardless of physical form or characteristics,
3. made or received
4. by any public or private institution
5. in pursuance of its legal obligations or in connection with the transaction of its proper business
6. and preserved or appropriate for preservation
7. by that institution or its legitimate successor
8. as evidence of its functions, policies, decisions, procedures, operations, or other activities or because of the informational value of the data contained therein.

The definition begins (element 1) by listing a few types of "documentary materials," which may reasonably be shortened to "documents." Evidently, Schellenberg means to suggest that records comprise all documents of whatever type and (element 2) whatever physical form—including, presumably, electronic records, paper, microforms, and so on. Elements 3, 4, and 5 and elements 6, 7, and 8 form two parallel groups. The first group relates to the creation of documents; the second relates to their preservation. The three elements within each group deal with three aspects of creation and preservation: the nature of each activity, its purpose, and the agent who performs it. Elements 3 and 6 deal with the nature of the activity, elements 4 and 7 deal with the agent, and elements 5 and 8 deal with the purpose. The particular activities that set records apart from other species of documents are (element 3) creation or receipt and (element 6) preservation ("appropriate for preservation" presumably includes documents that may not but should have been preserved). The agent of creation and receipt (element 4) is an institution, not an individual, but the nature of the institution is considered irrelevant. The institution is at the same time (element 7) the agent of preservation ("legitimate successor" presumably referring to a successor that continues the mandate and functions of the original agency). The reasons for creation (element 5) are either legal or functional and, for preservation (element 8), either evidential or informational.

It should be noted that, for Schellenberg, creation and preservation of a certain kind—as spelled out in elements 3 through 8—provide the sufficient conditions, as opposed to the necessary conditions, for the existence of records. In the present context, this familiar distinction can best be applied by recalling that Schellenberg first implies, in elements 1 and 2, that it is *necessary* for the material to have a documentary quality before it can be deemed *record* material or records. The material must necessarily have this quality to qualify as records, because a record is a special kind of document. All records are necessarily documents, but not all documents are necessarily records. By contrast, the qualities sufficient to qualify the documents as records—sufficient to distinguish them from other kinds of documents—are creation and preservation.[19]

Since all the elements of the definition have been brought together by distinguishing necessary from sufficient conditions, the definition can now be restated as follows: records are documents made or received by an institution according to law or its particular mandate and preserved by that institution as evidence or information.

Schellenberg's definition of records bears a family resemblance to a number of definitions of *archives* set down by earlier and later archivists. Among others one might note, consider the following:

> The whole of the written documents, drawings and printed matter, officially received or produced by an administrative body or one of its officials, in so far as those documents were intended to remain in the custody of that body or of that official (Muller, Feith, and Fruin, 1898)

> [Documents] drawn up or used in the course of an administrative or executive transaction (whether public or private) of which [they] formed a part; and subsequently preserved in their own custody for their own information by the person or persons responsible for that transaction and their legitimate successors (Hilary Jenkinson, 1922)

> The orderly accumulation of documents which were created in the course of its activity by an institution or an individual, and which are preserved for the accomplishment of its political, legal, or cultural purposes by such an institution or individual (Eugenio Casanova, 1928)

> All documents of all kinds which accrue naturally and organically as a result of the functions and activities of any administrative organization, body or individual...and which are kept for reference purposes (Michel Duchein, 1977).

These definitions of archives differ to some degree in detail and emphasis.[20] Still, without stopping to analyze them in depth, one might note that they do not differ significantly on fundamentals. They all emphasize creation and preservation and hence are compatible with Schellenberg's definition of records.

However, when defining archives, Schellenberg parts company with the traditional definitions cited above. He splits archives off from records by defining them as a species of records. Having defined records, he goes on to define archives as follows.

Those records of any public or private institution which are adjudged worthy of permanent preservation for reference and research purposes and which have been deposited or have been selected for deposit in an archival institution.[21]

Before examining this definition, a possible misunderstanding should be addressed. At first glance, it might be thought that extended consideration of the relation between the traditional definition of archives (or records) and the one formulated here by Schellenberg is beside the point, because archivists today generally use the term *records* when writing inventories of archival material. It can be agreed that the term *records* is generally so used.[22] However, two basic questions remain unanswered. First, what do archivists really mean when they use the term *records* in this way? Second, is that meaning the best possible formulation? In other words, the simple fact that a particular term is used tells one very little about what that term is supposed to mean, let alone whether that meaning is the best possible. Only by extrapolating from unexamined theoretical premises can one assume that such usage has a particular meaning and significance. Hence, the concern here with opening up such questions for examination.

As with his definition of records, Schellenberg's definition of archives can be conveniently set out in point form.

1. Those records
2. of any public or private institution
3. which are adjudged worthy of preservation
4. for reference and research purposes
5. and which have been deposited or have been selected for deposit in an archival institution.

This definition begins, with element 1, by simply pointing back to the earlier definition of records, which Schellenberg now proceeds to narrow. Element 2 is redundant, since it has already been included in the definition of records. Applying once again the distinction between necessary and sufficient conditions used to clarify his definition of records, elements 1 and 2 can be summed up by saying that their quality of being records provides the condition necessary for documents to be considered archives.

The conditions sufficient for them to be so considered are found in elements 3, 4, and 5. It will be noted that these three elements form a group that parallels the group of elements related to preservation in Schellenberg's definition of records.

As in the definition of records, these three elements deal with three aspects of preservation: the nature of the activity, its purpose, and the agent who undertakes it. Element 3 characterizes the activity not just as preservation, but as permanent preservation. Schellenberg adds the phrase "adjudged worthy," which was not included at the corresponding place in his definition of records, even though it is implicit in that definition (the phrase "*appropriate for preservation*" suggests that judgment precedes preservation). Element 4 characterizes the purpose of preservation in a slightly different way. Rather than point to the uses of the records (as evidence and information), he now refers to the activities of those who may use the records: reference and research. Element 5, also different, describes the agent of preservation not as the creating agency, but as a special archival institution in which records have been deposited, presumably transferred to from the creating agency ("selected for deposit" apparently referring to records in transit). Accordingly, his definition of archives may be restated as follows: archives are records judged worthy of permanent preservation for reference or research and deposited in an archival institution.[23]

Schellenberg's definitions of records and archives having thus been described and restated, it is now possible to explore his aim in splitting the two apart by looking at the differences between the definitions. As noted, there are four main differences with regard to preservation: records are preserved, but archives are permanently preserved; records are implicitly judged worthy of preservation, but archives are explicitly "adjudged worthy" of it; records are kept for evidence and information, but archives are kept for reference and research; records are kept by the creator, but archives are kept by an archival institution.

All these differences reflect Schellenberg's effort to define the archivist as the professional who selects documents used for administrative purposes and preserves them, mainly for scholarly use.[24] For example, records are preserved by the creator to accomplish the work for which they were created, which is assumed to have a limited time span, whereas archives are preserved permanently because scholars of all sorts may find any number of uses for them far into the future.[25] Moreover, archives are explicitly "adjudged worthy" of preservation, whereas records are not, in order to underscore the archivist's prime role in evaluating records for permanent preservation.[26] The somewhat confusing distinction between records kept for evidence and information and archives kept for reference and research is mainly intended to associate the word *research* with archives because, for Schellenberg, it is a synonym for "scholarly research."[27] Finally, records kept by the creator are distinguished from archives kept by an archival institution for two reasons: to underscore the distinction between the primary administrative and secondary scholarly reasons for preserving records; and to underscore the archivist's role in judging which records should be selected as archives.

Schellenberg's definitions of records and archives have been described and restated, and it has also been shown how the differences between the two relate to his aim in splitting archives from records. It now remains to investigate the reasons he gives in justification of his untraditional definition of archives. He offers two lines of argument in this regard.

The first line of argument Schellenberg offers to justify splitting archives from records is intended to support his twofold claim that "to be archives, materials must be preserved for reasons other than those for which they were created and accumulated" and that those reasons are mainly cultural.[28] In support of this claim, he offers two arguments from authority and one argument from the status quo.

First, he suggests that Jenkinson's definition of archives supports his own split between archives and records. Jenkinson, he notes, says that "records become archives when, 'having ceased to be in current use, they are definitely set aside for preservation, tacitly adjudged worthy of being kept.'" Still, having studied the English registry system, Schellenberg should have known better than to twist Jenkinson's meaning toward his own, however tempted he may have been. There is a touch of Old World charm (or magisterial condescension, depending on one's point of view) in Jenkinson's rejoinder, buried in a footnote, that this was merely "a slip" on Schellenberg's part, "justifying no more than a mild remonstrance." [29]

Schellenberg's second appeal to authority is a quote from the German archivist Brenneke. It is true, as Posner noted, that the

American and German definitions of archives stand together.[30] All the same, while arguments from authority were persuasive in medieval times, today we generally require reasoning based on propositions to justify a claim, especially when authorities disagree.[31]

Arguing as well from the status quo, Schellenberg claims that "it is quite obvious that modern archives are kept for the use of others than those that created them."[32] This claim would be quite obvious only if the National Archives of the United States—Schellenberg's employer, which did in fact keep archives for such uses—were the only archival institution housing modern archives. But archival institutions such as that of Illinois under the direction of Margaret Cross Norton kept archives primarily for the use of those who created them.[33] Still, even if all archival institutions housing modern archives did follow the National Archives of the United States, Schellenberg would not have substantiated his claim, because he is attempting to argue that what exists is what should exist, simply because it exists. To do so successfully, he would first have to demonstrate that terms such as *should* and *ought* are meaningless— which of course he does not do, because he uses them continually.[34] Clearly, Schellenberg has not adequately supported his claim that documents have to be preserved for secondary cultural reasons to be archives.

His second line of argument in justification of splitting archives from records is equally questionable. He argues that North American archivists should feel free to posit any view of archives they like because archivists everywhere have always defined archives with reference to their own particular needs.[35] This claim can be shown to be false by setting it out in syllogistic form.

a. All archivists define archives according to their own needs,
b. North American archivists need to select which records to preserve,
c. Therefore, North American archivists should define archives with the need for selection in mind.

If the first two elements of the argument are true, then the conclusion follows without question.

Consider the minor premise that North American archivists need to select records for preservation. They do, of course: legal obligations and the sheer bulk of documents require them to do so. But North Americans are not the only archivists in this position. Schellenberg argues to the effect that English archivists of the mid-twentieth century (and presumably their Continental peers— though perhaps not in Germany) were concerned solely with "the ancient public records." This claim is untrue. Jenkinson had gone on record in 1922 as a witness to the bulk of recent documents, devoting a large portion of his manual to a discussion of their selection and preservation.[36]

Schellenberg's major premise that all archivists define archives according to their particular needs is equally troublesome. True, all the definitions of archives noted above reflect differences in practice, but these differences in practice do not necessarily express differences in theory.[37] In fact, as expressions of theory, the definitions fit well with one another, for all of them emphasize both original use and preservation as the fundamental elements of archives. They differ somewhat in the way those fundamentals are expressed simply because they were framed within slightly different environments. To put it another way, these other archivists did not define archives according to their practical needs; rather, they defined the nature of archives in itself, though their different environments colored the way they formulated their definitions. The resulting differences are accidental, not essential, to the definitions. Schellenberg, however, confuses accidents with essences, missing entirely the agreement about fundamentals.

Since neither his major nor minor premise is defensible, Schellenberg fails to support his conclusion that North American archivists should define archives with the need for selection in mind. Since he also fails to support his claim that documents have to be preserved for secondary cultural reasons to be archives, both Schellenberg's lines of argument fail to support his untraditional definition of archives.

Aside from Schellenberg's own arguments, I have come across only two others offered in favor of his position. The first was succinctly phrased by Frank Evans, who thought the split between archives and records a good thing. As he put it, "to extend the meaning of archives back to records not yet appraised by the archivist and subject to disposition would be to involve the archivist in the destruction of archives."[38] It is true that archivists feel a strong responsibility about their role as the professionals designated to choose which documents to keep and which to destroy. Their age-old commitment toward preservation doubtless leads at times to some discomfort about destroying documents. P. Boisard, for example, found general agreement among Continental archivists that the "task of destroying records, which makes it necessary to make a selection (and selection always means the sacrifice of something else), gives archivists a most uncomfortable feeling."[39] All the same, they can at best only mask those feelings, not alleviate them, by changing the name of the material they destroy. Moreover, many archival institutions today are apparently destroying documents already in their care—archives, as defined by Schellenberg. For example, 65 percent of archival institutions responding to a recent Canadian national survey reported that they are actively involved in reappraising and "deaccessioning" (to a large extent destroying) material they had apparently once deemed worthy of permanent preservation.[40]

The other argument in support of Schellenberg's position claims that splitting archives from records is a good thing because of its administrative convenience.[41] In several respects, this claim is understandable. First, some aspects of the work done with documents in use by those who made or received them (commonly referred to as records management) will be different from work done with records that are used by others as well (commonly referred to as archives administration or management). Second, it may be useful, at least in large repositories, to have specialized staff for these somewhat different kinds of work. Third, it may be useful to have more than one program to accommodate those somewhat different kinds of work and to have that fact reflected in the organization's structure. Fourth, it may be convenient to have different names for those different programs.

Many institutions having two programs do, in fact, describe them as archives and records management or something similar. For administrative convenience, however, any names would do, as long as the programs are distinguished from one another. "Documents X management" and "documents Y management" would serve purely administrative concerns as well as any other names, because the logic of administrative convenience makes *any* choice of distinguishing names arbitrary. However, if the names given programs are arbitrary, they cannot be used to support Schellenberg's position, because no reasons relevant to a theoretical justification can be given for choosing one set of names over another; theory involves substantive, rather than nominal, definitions.[42] Even if administrators choose to employ Schellenberg's terms because they believe the concepts underlying them to be true, their choice cannot be used to buttress Schellenberg's claim, for they are *applying* his theoretical position to their own practical needs. An application of a theoretical claim assumes by definition that the claim is true, and therefore cannot be used to support it.[43]

As shown, the arguments of Schellenberg and others in defense of his split between archives and records are not persuasive. However, to demonstrate that his arguments do not substantiate his claim is not, in strict logic, to prove that his claim is false, because bad reasons can be given for a true proposition. One might, for example, argue that the sky is blue because "I say it is." The reason may persuade an over-docile dependent child, but not the rest of us, though we would have no trouble agreeing that the sky is, in fact, blue. To refute arguments in favor of a proposition is not to refute the proposition itself but to show that better reasons for believing the proposition are necessary.

To make this point clearer, consider an attempted refutation of Schellenberg's position that does not succeed but may nonetheless be true. Reviewing *Modern Archives*, Jenkinson attempted to prove that Schellenberg was wrong in order to defend the traditional view of archives, which treats *archives* and *records* as synonymous terms. Jenkinson urges that Schellenberg's definition of archives is "frankly arbitrary," going on to suggest that earlier definitions had been "based simply on an analysis of the nature of documents used in administration." Then he says

> Potential value for Research is no doubt the reason why we continue to spend time and money on preserving Archives and making them available: but the fact that a thing may be used for purposes for which it was not intended—a hat, for instance, for the production of a rabbit—is not part of its nature and should not, I submit, be made an element in its definition, though it may reasonably affect its treatment.[44]

This argument can be analyzed by using the syllogistic form employed earlier to examine one of Schellenberg's arguments:

a. Things should be defined according to their nature,
b. Uses for which things were not intended are not part of their nature,
c. Therefore, things should not be defined by uses for which they were not intended.

If the first two premises are true, then the conclusion follows without question.

The major premise—that things should be defined according to their nature—seems reasonable enough, but the minor premise is problematic. The difficulty lies in the notion of "intended uses" of things, because the concept is ambiguous. Jenkinson's rabbit-from-a-hat analogy—to which he likens Schellenberg's definition of archives as records used for purposes other than those for which they were first used—assumes that "intended uses" refers *only* to the original intention. Hats are originally made to be worn, and one finds it difficult to imagine any other use that might fittingly be made part of their definition. But the use originally intended is not always the only legitimate "intended" use. Schellenberg could, quite logically, reply that archives are not so much like hats as like an old pair of blue jeans; they may no longer be fit for wearing, but may still be used for rags. In so replying, he would simply be pointing out that the intended uses of some things can change over time, and it is his belief that records are exactly that sort of thing. They may be intended to be used first of all for administrative purposes by those who created them, he would urge, but after they have served those purposes, the equation of first use with intended use no longer applies. It is their second use by scholars—very much "intended"—that actually provides them with their archival quality.

By thus clarifying, or at least restating, his position, Schellenberg would show that Jenkinson begs the question. Jenkinson assumes, in his notion of intended use, an answer to the question at issue: which possible "intended" use of records—original or secondary—provides the best definition of archives? He assumes in his formulation of the question (the rabbit-from-a-hat analogy) that the original use is the only possible way of talking about "intended" use, and therefore does not allow Schellenberg a chance. The game is won before it is ever played, because Jenkinson does not argue directly against Schellenberg's claim. He assumes, rather, in his formulation of the question, that his is the only possible answer. Jenkinson's counterargument is therefore flawed and decides nothing.[45]

It has been seen so far that Schellenberg's untraditional definition of archives is neither refuted by Jenkinson's counterargument nor supported by the arguments offered in its favor, though it still remains conceivably true on purely logical grounds. This logic also holds for Jenkinson's counterargument, for while his question-begging does not demonstrate his point, neither does it show that he is wrong, let alone that Schellenberg is therefore right. Once again, bad reasons can be given for a true proposition.

Given these considerations, it might seem natural to proceed by asking whether Schellenberg's definition is in fact true or false, especially on the assumption that if Schellenberg's definition is right, then Jenkinson's must be wrong, and vice versa. Such a procedure would ill serve the discussion, because it involves two false assumptions: that the two definitions are mutually exclusive by necessity—that only one can be true and the other must be false—and that its truth is a sufficient condition for accepting one definition over another. A brief examination of these assumptions will point toward a more satisfactory method of continuing the discussion of Schellenberg's split between archives and records.

The assumption that the definitions are mutually exclusive by necessity is false, because more than one definition of a thing can be true. This is not to suggest that truth is relative, but that the world is complex. The thing defined possesses many qualities, attributes, or traits that may be emphasized or ignored by different definitions of it, and the definitions will all be true as long as they point to actual traits. A cat, for example, can be defined both as "a furry independent pet that mews" and as "a domesticated carnivorous mammal with retractile claws."[46] Both are true statements because both point to actual qualities. In this sense, both Schellenberg's and Jenkinson's definitions are true. Jenkinson's definition of archives, like Schellenberg's of records, emphasizes the original use and preservation of documents, whereas Schellenberg's emphasizes their selection and secondary use. All of these qualities can be predicated of the documents in question.[47]

The assumption that its truth alone is a sufficient condition for accepting one definition over another is also false, because definitions can have different contexts deriving from the purposes for which they are framed. There is at times a temptation to simply insist that one definition or another captures what Aristotle calls the "essence" of the thing defined and is therefore the real or the truer definition.[48] However, attributes essential for one purpose of defining a thing are not essential for other purposes. For example, the essential qualities of cats, as defined for everyday purposes, would likely include the fact that they are pets, are independent, and mew. By contrast, the essential qualities of cats, as defined for the purpose of developing a zoological classification scheme, would likely include the fact that they are mammals, as well as carnivores, are domesticated, and have retractile claws. Each of these true definitions is more acceptable than the other in its own context. It follows that if two definitions exist within the same context—are both, for instance, constructed for the purpose of developing a zoological classification scheme—then one is more acceptable than the other to the degree that it better suits that context. One can therefore say that the truth of a definition is a necessary, not a sufficient, condition for its acceptance over another. To be accepted over another, a definition must not only be true but also more suitable in a given context, which derives from the purpose for which it is framed.

Assuming, then, that the best procedure for examining a definition is to ask whether it is both true and suitable in its context, the discussion of Schellenberg's split between archives and records can be furthered accordingly. First of all, Schellenberg's untraditional definition is, as noted, true. Both of the attributes that he emphasizes—selection and secondary use—can be predicated of the documents in question. Jenkinson, for instance, accepts these as actual traits, although he does object to Schellenberg's emphasizing them. The main question about Schellenberg's definition of archives is how well it suits its context. This notion of a definition's context derives from the purpose for which it is intended, and should not be equated with the aim or purpose of the person who first framed the definition. Schellenberg's stated aim was to define the archivist as the professional responsible for selecting documents, mainly for scholarly research, in order to control the bulk of recent material.[49] However, the degree to which his definition may have served that aim is irrelevant to the present discussion, for the context here is archival theory. The attempt here is to provide a theoretical account of the nature of archives, and Schellenberg's definition must therefore be examined to find out how satisfactory a theoretical account it provides.[50]

An ideal theoretical account in any field of knowledge involves several elements, and any given bit of theory comes closer to that ideal as it embodies them. One of those elements—the only one needing mention for now—is the ideal of simplicity. This concept, otherwise known as Ockham's Razor or the principle of parsimony, can be stated in several ways. As a maxim, it reads: "entities are not to be multiplied beyond necessity"; "what can be done with fewer is done in vain with more"; "multiplicity is not to be assumed without necessity."[51] It is the principle by which scientists prefer the more "elegant" of two theories that fully account for the same phenomena—the one having the fewest assumptions or making the fewest moves in its argument.[52] Applied to the present discussion, the principle of simplicity can be stated as follows: if two definitions fully account for the same phenomena, the one that does so by relying on the fewest assumptions provides the better theoretical account.

As shown, Schellenberg first defines records in terms virtually identical with the traditional definition of archives, assuming that both cover the same ground. He then takes the further step of redefining archives, claiming that his definition takes account of two recent phenomena that the traditional definition ignores: the selection of documents for continued preservation by the archivist; and the use of those selected documents by persons other than those who first accumulated them in the course of their daily business. However, a closer look will show that the traditional definition is, in fact, powerful enough to account for both selection and secondary use, at least given a liberal interpretation of that definition.

Since Schellenberg's definition of records is virtually identical with the traditional definition of archives, and has already been analyzed, it may be used as a convenient model for reviewing the traditional concept of archives.[53] As noted earlier, Schellenberg's definition of records contains two three-element components dealing with the activity, the agent, and the purpose of both creation and preservation. Moreover, the three-part component dealing with preservation is paralleled in his definition of archives. As well, his definition of archives refers to records "adjudged worthy" of permanent preservation, a phrase excluded from but implicit in the parallel component of his definition of records.[54]

If the notion of judgment is implicit in the idea of this *first* preservation—if a moment of judgment exists between the moments of creation and preservation in a document's office of origin—then the original preservation of archives as traditionally defined logically implies that the documents have been *selected* for preservation in the office of origin. Between the judgment that a document is worthy of preservation and the decision to preserve it must come a moment when that judgment is confirmed. That confirmation implies selection. This apparent discovery, however, is little more than an exposure of the logic undergirding a claim once made by Jenkinson. As he put it, "every document which is preserved has been subject to [selection] at some stage (or even some stages) in its early career when for administrative reasons it was consigned to the file as an alternative to the waste-paper basket."[55]

Since selection for preservation thus takes place in the office where documents originate, the element of selection in Schellenberg's definition of archives is clearly not in itself what sets it apart from the traditional definition (or his own definition of records). What sets it apart are answers to three questions that sharpen the unqualified notion of selection:

1. By whom are the documents selected, the creator or the archivist?
2. For whom are they selected, the creator or the researcher?
3. For what purpose are they selected, administrative or cultural?

These three questions refine the three-part structure of the preservation component of Schellenberg's definitions of records and archives: activity, agent, and purpose. This component having been restated as "selection for preservation," the *activity* of selection has now been divided into (1) the agent, (2) the recipient, and (3) the purpose. This procedure brings together the phenomena of selection by the archivist and use by persons other than the creator, which makes it possible to view them as complementary aspects of a single phenomenon.[56] These questions, closely bound to one another, are brought together implicitly in Schellenberg's definitions of records and archives.[57] With records, on the one hand, (1) the creator selects (2) for his own (3) administrative use. With archives, on the other hand, (1) the archivist selects (2) for researchers' (3) cultural use.

Because the three elements in each definition are so closely bound to one another, it will be best to examine them in a way that covers them all at the same time. This can be done by first recalling that Schellenberg distinguishes between two basic sorts of value according to which documents are selected for preservation—primary and secondary. Though somewhat ambiguous at times, "primary" for Schellenberg generally means "first in time," referring to the values documents have for the creator in carrying out his everyday business. Primary values therefore include such things as administrative, operational, fiscal, and legal values. Secondary values, by contrast, are those that documents have for persons other than those who created them, and who put them to different uses. The two basic kinds of secondary value are evidential and informational. The former refers to documents that provide evidence about the structure of an organization and the manner in which it operated, while the latter refers to information in the documents about persons, things, and phenomena.[58] Schellenberg would say, then, that whereas records are selected for preservation by the creator for his own administrative use because of their primary values, archives are selected by the archivist for researchers' cultural use because of their secondary values.

Looking at Schellenberg's definitions of records and archives with these distinctions between different kinds of value in mind, one notices several things. First of all, it is evident that no absolute temporal distinction exists between documents selected by the creator for his own administrative use and those selected by the archivist for researchers' cultural use. That is, no date line can be drawn before which documents have only primary values and after which they have only secondary values. Schellenberg draws the distinction between primary and secondary values a bit too sharply in arguing that secondary values "inhere in public records after their primary values have been exhausted."[59] Documents such as charters, constitutions, and bylaws, for example, though no doubt a small percentage of the whole, lose their primary value only when the organization ceases to exist.[60]

Bearing in mind Schellenberg's distinction between the different values of documents, one also notices that no absolute distinction exists between the users of documents. Although the administrator may be most concerned with primary values and the scholar with informational values, both are concerned with evidential values. As Schellenberg himself points out, the scholar may use the documents to write a history of the organization, while the administrator may use them to recall precedents, solve problems, provide continuity, and prove his "faithful stewardship of the responsibilities delegated" to him.[61]

Another thing one notices—and it relates to both the foregoing observations—is that documents have both primary and secondary values from the moment of creation. Neither of Schellenberg's distinctions—the temporal or the one between users—takes into account the fact that secondary values exist for journalists, scholars, and citizens long before documents are transferred, if at all, to an archival repository. In fact, the journalist's hunger for a "scoop," like the concerned citizen's watchful eye, amply demonstrates that documents are laden with potential evidence and information for such groups from the very moment they are created or received.

This is not to say that these groups are necessarily in a position to exploit those secondary values. After all, numerous restrictions can exist on access to documents transferred to an archival repository, let alone those still used for administrative purposes in the office of origin. The point is not that these groups *can* exploit those values. The point, rather, is that they *could* do so, given a liberal enough access policy, because secondary values do exist potentially from the moment of a document's creation or receipt, if not sooner.

These inherent secondary values may have been less evident when Schellenberg wrote in 1956 than they are today. Now that access to information laws acknowledge the right of citizens to consult certain documents still in use by administrators, we are beginning to witness in practice the exploitation of secondary values that exist whether or not the documents are routinely open to inspection. Clearly, time and circumstance are not necessarily the theorist's allies. While the division between primary and secondary values has always been theoretically tenuous, though never noted as such, it is now coming to be recognized as "decidedly fuzzy," even in practice.[62]

Three main observations have been made so far regarding Schellenberg's distinctions between (a) records selected for preservation by the creator for his own administrative use because of their primary values and (b) archives selected by the archivist for researchers' cultural use because of their secondary values. First, the archivist is charged with the preservation of some documents with administrative value to the creator. Second, both creator and researcher exploit evidential values, the former for administrative and the latter for cultural reasons. And, third, all documents used by the creator for administrative purposes have secondary values for researchers and citizens. A further observation also follows from the secondary values inhering in documents from the moment of creation: the archivist's selection of documents for continued preservation is not the critical factor in determining which documents with secondary values will, in fact, become exploitable by researchers—or when. It is a matter of law or institutional policy whether or not documents still in use for administrative purposes by the creator may also be exploited for their secondary values by others—and when.

Schellenberg's distinction between records and archives can doubtless be modified and qualified enough to incorporate these observations, just as medieval astronomers could add epicycles to the Ptolemaic system in order to save the appearances. The same result can be achieved more simply by making three straightforward moves: (1) setting aside Schellenberg's idiosyncratic definition of archives; (2) equating his definition of records, in broad outline, with the traditional definition of archives; (3) restating the traditional definition of archives as "documents made or received in the course of the conduct of affairs and *preserved*." Selection is implicit in the notion of preservation. By leaving it implicit—by refraining from qualifying the notion of preservation—this reformulation of the traditional definition can accommodate, albeit tacitly, both the "records" and the "archives" sides of Schellenberg's distinctions between the agents, the recipients, and the purposes of selection for preservation.

More could be said at this point about the greater simplicity, flexibility, and theoretical potential that this version of the traditional definition has in comparison with Schellenberg's split between archives and records. However, it should suffice to note two further corollaries of his separation of the one from the other. First of all, consider the results for archival studies. Given Schellenberg's definitions, archival studies splits into two sorts of study—archival studies and record studies. Major components of archival studies would go to both of these areas, although archival studies would be, in some important respects, subordinate to and dependent on record studies. For example, archival studies would embody the theory, methodology, and practice of appraisal, reference, and probably acquisition and accessioning—all deriving from the definition of archives.

But some major portions of what was archival studies would shift to record studies. Among other things, the theoretical component of record studies would include all analyses of the qualities inhering in bodies of documents from the circumstances of their original accumulation and preservation, such as impartiality, authenticity, naturalness, and interrelatedness—all of which derive from the definition of records. Accordingly, the principles of provenance and original order, which are fundamental to archivists' methodology for arranging and describing documents and derive from the theoretical analysis of records, would have no basis in *archival* theory. In other words, the fundamental methodological principles underlying arrangement and description, often regarded as the heart of archivists' practical work, would properly form part of the separate science or discipline of record studies—even though formulated, elaborated theoretically, and used exclusively by archivists.

The other corollary of the split between archives and records is that the concept (or concepts) represented by these terms—the basic theoretical construct of archival studies (or record studies, or both)—becomes less stable, given Schellenberg's definition of archives. This instability can be seen from several angles. For one thing, if secondary use is a primary element in the definition of archives, then archives have only existed during the nineteenth and twentieth centuries, collaterally with the development of modern documentary history, and only in those places where such uses of documents are considered primary. Accordingly, none of the documents accumulated in the course of its business and preserved by the United States government were archives until the 1934 creation of the National Archives, from which time we may date their preservation for scholarly use, as opposed to their incidental prior preservation by bureaucrats. But this is not completely accurate,

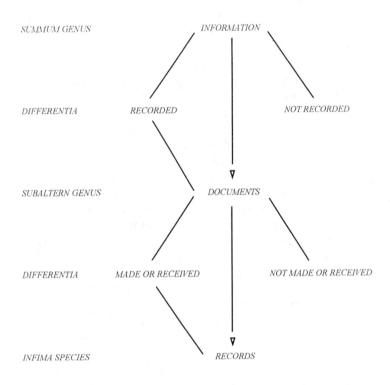

Figure 3. Archival Tree of Porphyry

for one would also have to say that United States government documents gathered by manuscript collectors and arranged in artificial groupings for historical research during the last two centuries *are* archives, at least if preserved in a repository calling itself an archives. It would also follow that repositories like that of the State of Illinois under the direction of Margaret Cross Norton which kept documents primarily for the use of those who created them, are not archival repositories and do not house archives— even though the material in the stacks at both Illinois and the National Archives might not turn out to be all that different in form and function.[63] Also, the archives at the National Archives could again become records with a change of policy, as the records of Illinois could become archives if that institution changed its policy.

Given the principle of simplicity, the ease with which the traditional definition of archives can accommodate the phenomenon of secondary use, and the complexity, instability, and perhaps even contradictions arising from Schellenberg's split between archives and records, it is difficult to avoid the conclusion that records are best defined—at least for purposes of archival theory—as archives in the traditional sense: documents made or received in the conduct of affairs and preserved.[64]

The two main definitions of records familiar to archivists today having been examined, the results can be summarized briefly by placing them within the logical hierarchy of archival terms introduced earlier. At the top of the hierarchy is the genus "information," defined as "intelligence given." The only species of information considered directly is documents, differentiated from all other species of information by having the quality of being recorded. "Documents" in turn becomes a genus for the species of documents called records, which are differentiated from all other species of documents by having the quality of being "made or received in the course of the conduct of affairs and preserved"; that is, by being "archival" in the traditional sense.[65] These relationships are set down graphically in Figure 3 according to a format traditionally known as the Tree of Porphyry.[66]

NOTES

1. Partridge, *Origins*, p. 555; Shipley, *Dictionary of Word Origins*, p. 298; *Oxford English Dictionary* 13: 359-62. So that the reader may refer to them

conveniently, and because of their generally high quality, all definitions in the several paragraphs that follow, except where noted, will be found in the *Oxford English Dictionary* hereafter cited as *OED*.

For the general interplay among English, French, and Latin, see Frederick Pollock and Frederic William Maitland, *The History of English Law Before the Time of Edward I*, 2nd ed., 2 vols. Cambridge: Cambridge University Press, 1968), 1: 80-87.

2. Although *memory* is the more common term, *recollection* is used here to point to the element of choice implicit in the idea. Memory can be involuntary, whereas recollection suggests something more deliberate. As well, *recollection* better embodies the ambiguity in this root meaning between memories that are distinctly personal or subjective and those that have a social or objective quality, simply because they are shared with others.

3. *OED*, which cites mainly jurists such as Coke and Blackstone, as well as legislation. See also *Black's Law Dictionary*, 6th ed. (St. Paul, MN: West Publishing Co., 1990), pp. 1273-74; and William Holdsworth, *A History of English Law*, 3rd ed., 16 vols. (London: Methuen, 1944), 9: 148.

4. *OED*, which cites mainly writers such as Shakespeare and Tennyson. Although the examples given date back only to the beginning of the seventeenth century, a related definition lists examples going back to the fourteenth century. It reads as follows: "the fact or condition of being preserved as knowledge, especially by being put in writing," as in phrases like "on record" ("knowledge" here referring to things "known" in the sense of "capable of being acknowledged").

5. M. T. Clanchy, *From Memory to Written Record: England 1066-1307*, 2nd ed. (Oxford: Blackwell, 1993), pp. 77, 254-55, 272-74, 295-96. According to Pollock and Maitland, the oldest records of this sort still in existence date from the end of the twelfth century (*History of English Law*, 1: 169).

6. J. H. Baker, *An Introduction to English Legal History*, 2nd ed. (London: Butterworths, 1979), p. 152.

7. William Lambarde, *Eirenarcha* (London, ca. 1600), cited in F. S. Thomas, *Notes of Materials*, p. 113. It is in this sense that certain judges in English cities or boroughs, and in some American states, are still called recorders. Originally the title denoted a legally knowledgeable person appointed "to 'record' or keep in mind the proceedings of [the] court and the customs of the city, his oral statement of these being taken as highest evidence of fact" (*OED*; *Black's Law Dictionary*, p. 1275).

8. Clanchy, *From Memory to Written Record*, pp. 266-72, 278-83. M. T. Clanchy, "Remembering the Past and the Good Old Law," *History* 55 (1970): 165-76.

9. Although some commentators have emphasized the differences between oral and written records, quite rightly in some respects, one may suspect that the evidence arrayed by Clanchy and others points to a large

measure of continuity between the two, as well—what one might in fact construe as functional equivalence (see, for instance, Hugh Taylor, "'My Very Act and Deed': Some Reflections on the Role of Textual Records in the Conduct of Affairs," *American Archivist* 51 [Fall 1988]: 456-69).

10. Frank B. Evans, Donald F. Harrison, and Edwin A. Thompson, comps., "A Basic Glossary for Archivists, Manuscript Curators, and Records Managers," *American Archivist* 37 (July 1974): 428. See also Mary F. Robek, Gerald F. Brown, and Wilmer O. Maedke, *Information and Records Management*, 3rd ed. (Encino, CA: Glencoe Publishing Company, 1987), p. 4. Although this definition of records does not appear in Bellardo and Bellardo's recent *Glossary for Archivists*, that does not necessarily mean that it has become obsolete, for the compilers do not always or clearly distinguish whether they are attempting to describe or prescribe usage (see, in this regard, the review of this work by Terry Eastwood in *American Archivist* 55 [Summer 1992]: 493-96). However, even if this definition of records has in fact become obsolete—and the *Glossary* actually prefers the term *document* for this usage, as argued for as well below—the present discussion may be viewed as providing some of the reasons why it has *rightly* become so.

11. Those considering such matters in greater detail may wish to consult Helmut Felber, *Terminology Manual* (Paris: UNESCO, General Information Programme and UNISIST/Infoterm, 1984).

12. In traditional terms, "recorded information" is thus a "complete" or workable definition of records. According to Aristotle, a complete definition must possess at least two terms: one that incorporates the genus-species relationship, and one that incorporates the attribute that differentiates the species in question from all others (see Cohen and Nagel, *An Introduction to Logic*, pp. 235-36).

It will have been noticed that while the only species of information given for purposes of the present definition is records, at least two species of information are tacitly assumed to exist—recorded and *un*recorded. Any given differentiating attribute logically implies at least one other: its contradictory. However, unrecorded information is left undefined in the archival literature, perhaps for the sensible reason that the authors are interested only in defining terms of direct archival relevance.

13. For a more rigorous explication of this distinction, though in a slightly different context, see note 19 below.

14. Fritz Machlup, "Semantic Quirks in Studies of Information," in *The Study of Information: Interdisciplinary Messages*, ed. Fritz Machlup and Una Mansfield (New York: John Wiley & Sons, 1983), p. 653. Thoughtful commentary on this term and the circumstances involved in its meteoric rise in status will be found in Roszak, *The Cult of Information*; and Joseph Weizenbaum, *Computer Power and Human Reason: From Judgment to Calculation* Harmondsworth, England: Penguin, 1984). Ample evidence of the

confusion over the term among those involved in information science itself is provided in Christopher John Fox, *Information and Misinformation: An Investigation of the Notions of Information, Misinformation, Informing, and Misinforming* (Westport, CT: Greenwood Press, Contributions in Librarianship and Information Science No. 45, 1983), pp. 39-74. Among archivists, the term has been defined at least once—in Peter Walne, ed., *Dictionary of Archival Terminology* (Munich: K. G. Saur, 1984). Unfortunately, this compilation (which relates terms hierarchically in the order of data / information / documents / records / archives) is somewhat inconsistent, though it nonetheless merits scrutiny by those interested in devising a workable hierarchy of terms for archival use.

15. Samuel Johnson, *A Dictionary of the English Language...* (London: W. Strathams, 1755). This definition is referred to in Basil Stuart-Stubbs, "Keynote Address: Whither Information?" in Cynthia J. Durance, comp., *Management of Recorded Information: Converging Disciplines; Proceedings of the International Council on Archives' Symposium on Current Records; National Archives of Canada, Ottawa, May 15-17 1989* (Munich: K. G. Saur, 1990), p. 16.

16. Luciana Duranti, "Diplomatics: New Uses for an Old Science," *Archivaria* 28 (Summer 1989): 15.

17. The equation of "documents" with both "recorded information" and "records" will be found in Evans, Harrison, and Thompson, "Glossary," p. 421. As indicated in note 10 above, Bellardo and Bellardo's *Glossary for Archivists*, like the present study, equates only "documents" and "recorded information."

18. Schellenberg, *Modern Archives*, p. 16.

19. The distinction between necessary and sufficient conditions can be stated formally as follows: "a proposition p states a *sufficient condition* for another proposition q if 'p implies q' is true. A proposition p states a *necessary condition* for another proposition q if '$not\text{-}p$ implies $not\text{-}q$' is true (or what is the same thing, if 'q implies p' is true)" (Cohen and Nagel, *An Introduction to Logic*, p. 388). In terms of the present discussion, the relevant propositions for a necessary condition would be, p, "This is a document," and q, "This is a record." For a sufficient condition, the relevant propositions would be, p, "This is a document with the qualities outlined in elements 3 through 8," and q, "This is a record."

20. The first three definitions are given as cited in Schellenberg, *Modern Archives*, p. 12. The last one is from Michel Duchein, "The Principle of Provenance in Archives Administration," in *Modern Archives Administration and Records Management: A RAMP Reader*, ed. Peter Walne (Paris: UNESCO, General Information Programme and UNISIST, 1985), p. 85.

21. Schellenberg, *Modern Archives*, p. 16. Some idea of the range of influence this definitional split has had will be found in Clive Smith, "Glossary of Terminology," in *Keeping Archives*, ed. Ann Pederson (Syd-

ney: Australian Society of Archivists, 1987), pp. 357, 364. See also the exchange of views between Commonwealth archivists in *Archives* 7 (April 1965: 57-58; October 1965: 93-94; April 1966: 163-66; October 1966: 237).

22. See, for example, the list of inventories in National Archives and Records Administration, *Select List of Publications of the National Archives and Records Administration* (Washington, DC: National Archives and Records Administration, General Information Leaflet No. 3, 1986), pp. 6-16. *Records* is also the preferred term, either explicitly or by implication, in the three main English-language sets of rules for description in use today: Bureau of Canadian Archivists, *Rules for Archival Description;* Michael Cook and Margaret Procter, *A Manual of Archival Description,* 2nd ed. (Aldershot, England: Gower Publishing Company, 1989); and Steven L. Hensen, *Archives, Personal Papers, and Manuscripts: A Cataloging Manual for Archival Repositories, Historical Societies, and Manuscript Libraries,* 2nd ed. (Chicago: Society of American Archivists, 1989).

23. With regard to the activities of reference and research, "or" is a better combining term than "and" for two reasons. First, "or" generally implies "and" in standard English usage (Wilson Follett, *Modern American Usage: A Guide,* ed. Jacques Barzun [New York: Hill & Wang, 1966], pp. 64-65). Second, it would be best to avoid the possible assumption that only records useful for *both* reference and research would qualify as archives. Schellenberg—to anticipate what follows—is trying to insinuate into his definition of archives the value of records for scholarly research above all else. Accordingly, while "and" may have been the best rhetorical form for his own purposes, "or" seems closer to his meaning.

24. Schellenberg, *Modern Archives,* p. 30; T. R. Schellenberg, "Principles of Archival Appraisal," in *Modern Archives Administration,* ed. Walne, pp. 269, 270.

25. Schellenberg, *Modern Archives,* p. 110.

26. Ibid., p. 30.

27. Ibid., p. 140. Schellenberg's definition is confused, as well as confusing, at this point. With regard to records, he does not in fact state what he really means concerning the reasons for which records are preserved by the institution that created them. He *says* that they are preserved for evidence and information, but he actually means that they are preserved for administrative, legal, and fiscal purposes in order to carry out the institution's work. This intent becomes clear later on in his discussion of appraisal, where he distinguishes the primary administrative, legal, and fiscal values of records—values for the creator—from their secondary evidential and informational values for scholarly research above all else. He continually connects the uses of records as evidence and information with the activities of reference and research (noting that their occasional use in this way by the creating institution is not the same as their first use in accomplishing the institution's work). Accordingly, he clearly means to

define records as "documents made or received by an institution according to law or its particular mandate and preserved to fulfill its administrative, legal, or fiscal needs." The correspondingly revised definition of archives would read, "records judged worthy of permanent preservation for reference or research use because of their evidence and information and deposited in an archival institution." This confusion is mainly verbal and does not affect the substance of the two definitions (see *Modern Archives*, pp. 133, 139-60).

28. Ibid., pp. 13, 14, 140.

29. Ibid., pp. 13-14; Hilary Jenkinson, "Modern Archives. Some Reflections on T. R. Schellenberg: *Modern Archives: Principles and Techniques*," in his *Selected Writings of Sir Hilary Jenkinson*, p. 340. It might also be noted that Schellenberg seems to have borrowed the peculiar phrase, "adjudged worthy," from Jenkinson.

30. Schellenberg, *Modern Archives*, p. 14; Posner, *Archives in the Ancient World*, p. 4.

31. C. S. Lewis, *The Discarded Image: An Introduction to Medieval and Renaissance Literature* (Cambridge: Cambridge University Press, 1964), p. 11.

32. Schellenberg, *Modern Archives*, p. 14.

33. Margaret Cross Norton, *Norton on Archives: The Writings of Margaret Cross Norton on Archival and Records Management*, ed. Thornton W. Mitchell (Carbondale: Southern Illinois University Press, 1975), pp. 4-5.

34. Examples of Schellenberg's normative language abound. See, for instance, *Modern Archives*, pp. 28, 29, 30.

35. Ibid., p. 15.

36. Ibid.; Jenkinson, *A Manual of Archive Administration*, pp. 21, 136-90.

37. It might be noted that all except the last of these definitions are cited by Schellenberg in defense of his position as set down here.

38. Frank B. Evans, "Modern Concepts of Archives Administration and Records Management," *UNESCO Bulletin for Libraries* 24 (1970): 244. The same argument was offered earlier by Arthur H. Leavitt, "What Are Archives?" *American Archivist* 24 (April 1961): 177.

39. P. Boisard, "Disposal Policy: Reflections on the Practice of the Archives of the Seine," in *Modern Archives Administration*, ed. Walne, p. 212.

40. National Archives of Canada, Program Evaluation and Research Policy Branch, *Acquisition Evaluation Study*, vol. 2, *Research Reports* (November 1987), pp. 9, 10. An argument in favor of reappraisal and deaccessioning will be found in Leonard Rapport, "No Grandfather Clause: Reappraising Accessioned Records," in *A Modern Archives Reader*, ed. Daniels and Walch, pp. 80-90.

41. Peter Walne, letter to the editor, *Archives* 7 (April 1966): 165; Ivor M. Graham, letter to the editor, *Archives* 7 (October 1966): 237.

42. Theory, that is, as understood for the purposes of this study. Nominal definitions are agreements about what specific words shall mean, whereas substantive definitions are propositions about the nature of things. Substantive definitions are mentioned, and a citation given, in Chapter 2, note 1, where a form of nominal definition relating to the use of "idea" is offered as well.

43. A common reason for administrators' choice of the terms *archives* and *records* to refer to their separate programs, one might suppose, is that attributed to Solon Buck, second archivist of the United States. According to H. G. Jones, Buck, like Jenkinson and Waldo G. Leland, strongly believed that records are in fact archives as traditionally defined. But he nonetheless agreed to use the term *records* because it was supposedly more easily understood by nonarchivists—and it was during his tenure as national archivist that *records administration* emerged (H. G. Jones, *The Records of a Nation: Their Management, Preservation, and Use* [New York: Atheneum, 1969], p. 36, note 25; p. 25). An example of Buck's equation of records and archives will be found in his "Let's Look at the Record," *American Archivist* 8 (April 1945): 110-11.

44. Jenkinson, "Modern Archives. Some Reflections on T. R. Schellenberg," *Journal of the Society of Archivists* 1 (April 1957): 148-49. Some five lines of this article, including most of the quote about the rabbit from a hat, have been omitted from the article as reprinted in Jenkinson's *Selected Writings* (p. 341), cited earlier. Accordingly, a double citation to the same article seems both useful and necessary.

45. Arguments formulated in the heat of battle are often similarly flawed. For example, two recent arguments seeking to undermine the view that archives can be defined by the scholarly uses to which they can be put also beg the question at issue. Both authors assume in their premises that things *cannot* be defined according to the criterion of use (taking a slightly different line of attack from Jenkinson, although toward the same end). But things like hats, blue jeans, rags, and tools of all sorts can clearly be so defined. The question that these authors beg is: are archives in fact things that can or cannot be defined by their uses? See Eastwood, "Nurturing Archival Education," p. 234; and Trevor Livelton, "Some Thoughts on the Archival Function and Method, With a Note on Their Relation to the Arsenal of the Forum" (term paper for ARST 500, School of Library, Archival and Information Studies, University of British Columbia, September 1988), pp. 4-6.

46. *Funk & Wagnalls Standard College Dictionary*, 1974 Canadian ed., s.v. "Cat."

47. The expression "Jenkinson's definition" is meant to refer to what has here been called the traditional view of archives, not Jenkinson's own formulation of it. His view that unbroken custody is essential to the definition of archives was directly attacked by Schellenberg (*Modern Ar-*

chives, pp. 14-15); and, while the controversy is of interest in its own right, it is irrelevant to the present discussion and is best ignored. In the present context, Jenkinson is but a symbol for the widely held view against which Schellenberg argues.

48. Cohen and Nagel, *An Introduction to Logic,* p. 235.

49. Schellenberg, *Modern Archives,* pp. 15-16.

50. It can be urged, in light of the view of archival theory underlying this study, that the definition of all basic concepts must finally have a purely theoretical context because a good many aspects of archival methodology, practice, and scholarship follow from the fundamental concepts that archivists adopt and the analyses they make of them. In other words, whatever aims underlie a particular definition of a basic concept, the ultimate justification of that definition must be theoretical. With regard to the definition of basic concepts, not all contexts are equal. Although this belief lies in the background here, a softer argument has been used in the text, for an ax need not be employed where a paring knife will do.

51. William L. Reese, *Dictionary of Philosophy and Religion: Eastern and Western Thought* (Atlantic Highlands, NJ: Humanities Press, 1980), s.v. "William of Ockham (8)." For a detailed discussion of what the term *simple* means in this context, and for examples of false simplicity, see Cohen and Nagel, *An Introduction to Logic,* pp. 212-15, 384-88.

52. Cohen, *Reason and Nature,* pp. 106-14. Cohen discusses simplicity as an element of the broader ideal of system, according to which, ideally, any given bit of theory is logically connected to every other bit of theory in the same field of knowledge, all of them together forming a cohesive and comprehensive whole—a system. He suggests, however, that even a syllogism can be considered a logical system of sorts, which implies that the ideal of system and the principle of simplicity can be applied both to the whole of a field of knowledge and to its parts. Considering the centrality of the definition of archives to the field of archival studies—considering, that is, how wide-ranging are the implications for the whole, depending on how this central part is framed—there has been no hesitation here to apply the principle of simplicity directly to the definition of archives, rather than take the circuitous route of first discussing the ideal of system in relation to archival studies as a whole.

53. On Schellenberg's definition of records, see pp. 63-65 above.

54. These parallels between Schellenberg's definitions of records and archives are described above at pp. 66-67.

55. Jenkinson, "Modern Archives," in his *Selected Writings,* pp. 340-41.

56. It should be noted that the distinction between documents selected for temporary or permanent preservation is ignored here, because it is subordinate to the question of the use or purpose for which they are selected. Documents are preserved for as long as they are of use, whatever that use might be. The term *permanent* is in any case ambiguous, at least

without some modifying context. *Permanent* suggests something close to "forever." Does this mean until the universe, our galaxy, our solar system, life on earth, the present geopolitical structure, ideological systems, or archival institutional policies cease to exist? Accordingly, as the reader will have noticed, the term *continued* has generally been used throughout this study in preference to "permanent" (cf. James M. O'Toole, "On the Idea of Permanence," *American Archivist* 52 [Winter 1989]: 10-25).

57. He brings them together implicitly, that is, in the definitions he offers formally. As pointed out in note 27 above, for instance, they would to some extent have been more explicit if Schellenberg had said what he actually meant.

58. T. R. Schellenberg, *The Appraisal of Modern Public Records* (Washington, DC: National Archives of the United States, Bulletin No. 8, 1956), pp. 6-7.

59. Schellenberg, "Principles of Archival Appraisal," in *Modern Archives Administration*, ed. Walne, p. 236.

60. Maygene F. Daniels, "Records Appraisal and Disposition," in *Managing Archives and Archival Institutions*, ed. James Gregory Bradsher (Chicago: University of Chicago Press, 1989), p. 61. Bodies of documents that were accumulated in the course of business by defunct organizations and have been acquired by a repository are, of course, unlikely to have any primary values. The discussion here, in line with Schellenberg, relates to an ongoing concern.

61. Schellenberg, *Modern Archives*, p. 140.

62. Jay Atherton, "From Life Cycle to Continuum: Some Thoughts on the Records Management-Archives Relationship," *Archivaria* 21 (Winter 1985-86): 47.

63. Compare Schellenberg, *Modern Archives*, pp. 139-60 with Norton, *Norton on Archives*, pp. 239-46.

64. Unfortunately, the focus of this study precludes a thorough discussion of the nature of records, which warrants an entire study in its own right, at the very least. In line with the broad theoretical considerations outlined here, this study foregoes the examination of important and difficult questions such as the status of electronic and three-dimensional records in order to draw attention to some overarching considerations. However, it may be of some use here to at least glance at the question of "nonrecords." From the standpoint of the argument developed so far, it follows that the distinction sometimes made between records and nonrecords is generally unwarranted, at least when the latter term is used to denote records used and preserved only temporarily (see Peterson and Peterson, *Law*, pp. 13-15). There are often difficult decisions to be made about the length of time different records should be kept. But this length of time does not enter into the definition of records, which requires only that documents be made or received and preserved, no matter how long.

These "nonrecords" are more properly dubbed "transitory records," as Peterson and Peterson note and as some organizations have done (ibid., p. 15; Province of British Columbia, B.C. Archives and Records Service, *Administrative Records Classification System* [Victoria, 1993], "Special Schedules," pp. 3-4).

65. The nature of manuscripts and papers, sometimes distinguished from records or documents, is discussed below in Chapter 5.

66. See Cohen and Nagel, *An Introduction to Logic,* p. 236. The preceding discussion would permit one to place "intelligence" at the top of the hierarchy in place of "information" and divide it into the differentia "given" and "not given." "Intelligence," however, has been omitted from Figure 3 to keep the latter as clear and simple as possible.

Chapter 4

From Records to Public Records

Within the context of this study, discussion of the nature of public records can most usefully begin by placing that concept within the logical hierarchy of archival terms developed in the last chapter. Such a beginning will make for a fairly abstract discussion, which some readers may find tiresome. However, in taking time at the outset to place the concept of public records within the hierarchical structure developed earlier, two fundamental and interrelated tactical objectives will be gained. First, by focusing on the logic of the concept at the beginning, it should be possible to forestall to some extent the legitimate but potentially distracting concerns that archivists inevitably bring to such a discussion. Second, it will be discovered that the concept of public records has logical implications which, though generally overlooked, enable those pressing concerns to be focused more sharply and clearly.

PUBLIC RECORDS AND THE HIERARCHY OF TERMS

To begin with, it will be recalled that the last chapter ended by placing the two senses of the term *records*—as documents and archives—within a logical hierarchy of terms consisting of "intelligence," "information," "documents," and "records." It will also be recalled that the relations between those terms were drawn out by noting that, within this hierarchy, a specific adjective-noun relationship corresponds to each species-genus relationship. In particular, it was noted that a species is defined by combining a specific adjective with the noun representing that species' genus. Thus, for instance, documents—as a species of the genus information—was defined as "recorded information." The adjective *recorded,* combined with the noun *information,* yielded a full definition of documents. This combination yielded such a definition because *recorded,* while grammatically an adjective, is at the same time the logical connector between genus and species; it provides the differentiating attribute of the species documents that distinguishes the latter from all other species of the genus information.

Similarly, a step further down the hierarchy, the noun *documents* was in turn viewed as a genus in its own right. This particular noun/genus, when combined with the adjective phrase "made or received in the conduct of affairs and preserved," yielded the species records—the adjective phrase having differentiated records from all other species of the genus documents. By this method of relating adjectives and nouns to species and genera, it was possible to move downward through the hierarchy of terms, step by step. Each genus was connected with its subordinate species through the intermediate step of combining a specific adjective with the noun representing that genus.

It should not be assumed, however, that the simple fact of an adjective-noun relationship between the terms *public* and *records* necessarily implies the same logical relationship between a species and its genus. Adjectives and nouns can be related logically in more than this one particular way—however useful that relationship may have proved as a means of developing the hierarchy of archival terms set forth in the last chapter. In fact, by comparing the relationship between the adjective *public* and the noun *records* with that of the species-genus relationships developed in the last chapter, it can be shown that public records are best considered not so much a species, as a subspecies or *type* of records.

In the last chapter, information was defined as intelligence given, documents as recorded information, and records as documents made or received in the conduct of affairs and preserved. By so defining these terms, a consistent criterion for distinguishing a species from its genus was set down. When examined, it will be seen that all these definitions rest upon the distinction between a thing and an action or, more precisely, a thing differentiated from other similar things because it results from a particular action. A thing, information, is differentiated from other things resembling it—other species, that is, of the genus intelligence—by the action of "being given." A thing, documents, is likewise distinguished from other similar things—other species of the genus information—by the action of "being recorded." And a thing, records, is in the same manner distinguished from others resembling it—other species of the genus documents—by the action of "being made or received in the conduct of affairs and preserved." In each of these definitions, the quality represented by the adjective (as in "*recorded* information," when defining documents) refers to a specific kind of action that differentiates the species in question from all other species of the same genus.

However, the same relationship does not hold between the adjective *public* and the noun *records*. The conceptual move a step down the hierarchy from the thing, records, to the more specific thing, public records, does not involve an *action*. Intelligence is "given," information "recorded," and documents "made or received in the conduct of affairs and preserved." But *public* is an attribute which, in relation to the archival definition of records, does not represent a comparative action. As it qualifies the archival definition of records, *public* refers rather to a kind of person—to a specific type of actor responsible for the action of "making or receiving…" the documents defined as records. In moving from records to public records, in other words, a new term has been introduced to the discussion, inviting a new question: *who* has accomplished the action (of "making and receiving…") that distinguishes the thing, records, from other species of documents?

THE PERSON CRITERION

Before examining why this distinction between an action and the person who performs it leads to viewing public records as a subspecies or type of records, two prior questions must be addressed.

1. Should the concept of person be the criterion for dividing records into public records and other related subcategories?
2. Should the concept of person be limited to the actor who makes or receives and preserves documents?[1]

These questions are prior to the question of the status of public records in the hierarchy of terms (species or subspecies) because the formulation of the status question offered here assumes that the answer to both questions is yes. The first question refers to the suitability of the concept of person in general as the criterion for division, while the second question refers to the suitability of the particular definition of that concept employed here. Both questions will be briefly examined in turn.

The first question—about whether or not the concept of person should be the criterion for dividing records—hinges on the relationship between that concept and the hierarchy of terms so far developed. That hierarchy forms a logical system of terms, each of them connected to all the others as parts of a cohesive and comprehensive whole. Therefore, the question of whether or not the concept of person is a suitable criterion for dividing records depends on two things: whether that concept in fact fits within the system and, if it does fit within the system as a whole, whether it fits at this particular place in the system—that is, as a suitable criterion for dividing records.

Clearly, the concept of person does fit within the system of terms, for it is one of the characteristics that have tacitly been agreed on as relevant to the definition of those terms. It will be recalled, for example, from the analysis of Schellenberg's definition of records and the traditional definition of archives, that archivists have stressed at least five aspects of records when defining them: the nature of the material, its form, the action from which it results, the purpose of the action, and the person who performs that action.[2] Without weighing the relative importance of these several elements, they may be distinguished by repeating a traditional definition of archives. As Duchein puts it, archives are "all documents [the nature of the material] of all kinds [its form] which accrue naturally and organically as a result of the functions and activities [the action from which it results] of any administrative organization, body or individual [the person who performs that action]...and which are kept for reference purposes [the purpose of the action of preservation]."[3]

Moving a step up the hierarchy of terms from records to documents, only four of these five elements are directly relevant: the nature of the material, its form, the action from which it results, and the person who performs that action. The definition of documents as "recorded information" supplies two of these directly—"information" referring to the nature of the material and "recorded" to the action from which it results. But also included implicitly are the form of the material and the person who performs the action. There can be no action without an actor, and everything that is recorded must be recorded in some physical form. The definition does not include the purpose for which the person performs the action of recording. This is reasonable, however, since it was earlier demonstrated that the recording of information need not be a deliberate act.[4]

The definition of information, one step further up the hierarchy, includes only three of the five elements used in the definition of records: the nature of the material, the action from which it results, and the person who performs that action. If information is intelligence given, then both the nature of the material (intelligence) and the action from which it results (being given) are explicitly included. As with the definition of documents, the occurrence of an action also implies the presence of an actor. However, the presence of an actor does not imply a purpose. Nor, as demonstrated earlier, does the act of "giving" intelligence imply that the latter is embodied in a physical form.[5] Since the concept of person is thus a definitional element at each level of the hierarchy of terms, it clearly does fit within the system.

It also fits within the system as a suitable criterion for dividing records into public records. In fact, of the five characteristics identified as elements of the definition of records, the notion of person is the most reasonable candidate. The nature of the material is clearly an inappropriate criterion for dividing records, since records themselves must be considered the nature of the material in any definition of public records. The nature of the material is what is being divided, and it cannot therefore be the criterion for that division. The concept of form is inappropriate because it is counterintuitive. "Public records" simply does not parallel categories such as electronic records, video records, and paper records. The concept of purpose is also inappropriate because it is dependent on the prior existence of a person performing an action *for* a purpose. It cannot stand alone. The concept of action, by contrast, could conceivably fit. After all, "to publicize" (or "publish") is a recognizable verb meaning "to make public, bring before the public."[6] However, the notion of publication is dependent on first determining the nature of the public whom the records are brought before or made known to. In other words, this particular form of action, like the notion of purpose, is meaningful only in relation to a prior definition of the kind of person it implies: the public, whoever or whatever that may be.[7]

Accordingly, the concept of person remains the strongest candidate for the criterion used to divide records. The concepts of the nature of the material and its form are clearly inadequate, while the concept of person underlies the concepts of both purpose and action. It is hard to imagine the notion of person in itself offending anyone's intuitive sense of the kind of thing to which *public* refers.

A word of explanation is in order at this point, since readers may, at first glance, find this result somewhat at odds with the definition of records offered in the previous chapter. There, it will be recalled, three of the five elements of the definition were tacitly drawn out for extended scrutiny on the assumption that they deal with the heart of the matter—the nature of the material, the action from which it results, and the purpose of that action. Records, accordingly, were defined as "documents [the nature of the material] made or received in the course of the conduct of affairs [the action from which it results] and preserved [a further action that entails the several purposes subsumed under what is usually referred to as 'evidence and information']." Excluded from primary consideration were the elements of form and person. It was assumed that neither the medium in which they are embodied nor the nature of the person who makes or receives them has any essential bearing on the fundamental nature of records.

Although this statement may not raise many eyebrows today, many archivists in the past have believed that the nature of the person generating records has an essential bearing on their fundamental nature. Schellenberg, for instance, restricts his definition of records to those documents made or received by "any public or private *institution*," thereby excluding physical persons from consideration. But the matter is more complex, for even Schellenberg devoted much of his later *Management of Archives* to erasing the distinction between various types of records creator.[8] Nonetheless, this statement may stand for present purposes, since it will be dealt with fully in due course.

In any case, recalling this tacit downplaying of the person element in the definition of records, one may wonder why it is here raised above the notions of action and purpose. The answer lies in the different purposes of the two analyses and the correspondingly different role played in each by the concept of person. This concept, though secondary for the purpose of *defining* records, is primary for the purpose of *dividing* records. Though the notion of person was of secondary importance in the chapter where the nature of records was at issue, it is of primary importance in this chapter, providing a bridge between the analysis of records and that of public records. The same concept may bear different amounts of weight, depending on the context in which it is employed. Even so, these different contexts are part of a whole, and do have some bearing on one another. Note, for instance, that while the notion of person may be of only secondary importance in the definition of records, its mere existence within that definition ensures that a division of records using the criterion of person is not at all arbitrary. Moreover, the mere fact that "public" is a type of records creator traditionally employed in the definition of archives or records—though generally not defined precisely (recall, for example, Duchein's definition)—further ensures that an acceptable subcategory of records has been chosen for examination, no matter how that subcategory may be defined substantively when the analysis is done.

Since the concept of person is in general terms an appropriate criterion for dividing records into public records and other similar subcategories, it is now necessary to determine whether the particular definition of that concept offered here is also appropriate. More specifically, should the concept of person be limited, as assumed here, to the actor who makes or receives and preserves documents?

First of all, to assume that the concept of person should be limited in this way to what may be called provenance is not to ignore alternative definitions of the concept.[9] It is, rather, to choose among those alternatives by following the logic inherent in the discussion so far. The alternatives are fairly clear. The law, for example, offers several possible ways of qualifying *person:* provenance in the legal sense ("proceeding from" the public); pertinence ("relating to" the public); effects ("affecting" the public); access ("open to" the public); and ownership ("belonging to" the public).[10] Intuitively, all these ways of limiting the concept of person have merit.

However, the logic of the discussion so far forces the issue: provenance is the only notion by which the concept of person can reasonably be limited or qualified. To understand why this is so requires a glance at both the goal of the present discussion and the means necessary to achieve it. The goal of the discussion is to logically divide records into its subcategories—in particular, to determine the nature of the subcategory called public records. The means to achieve that goal are several, but one of the most important is to determine an appropriate criterion on which to base the division and then to refine that criterion. Only by determining whether the criterion is appropriate can it be ensured that the division is sound, and only by refining that criterion can it be ensured that the division is precise. And, it may also be added, only by determining that the criterion so refined is consistent with the theoretical structure of which it forms a part can it be ensured that the resulting division of records conforms to the scientific ideal of system.

The appropriateness of the concept of person as a means of dividing records having been determined, it is now necessary to refine that concept by limiting or qualifying it. The claim that provenance is the only notion by which the concept of person can reasonably be qualified is based primarily on the need to maintain consistency within the theoretical structure developed in this study.[11] If the earlier definition of records as archives in the traditional understanding is acceptable, then it follows that the only reasonable basis for refining the concept of person as a criterion for dividing records is the notion of provenance *embedded within that definition*—at least if one values consistency. The notion of provenance forms an integral part of the structure so far developed, and it can only be abandoned at the cost of ignoring everything that has gone before. Accordingly, having determined that records are documents made or received and preserved by *someone*, there seems little reason for shifting toward some other qualifying notion of person, however intuitively plausible it might seem out of context. Other qualifying notions are certainly possible, logically. However, the burden of proof and what goes with it—specifically, an entirely new definition of records and an appropriate restructuring of the hierarchy of terms—naturally rests with any attempt to offer such alternative notions for rational consideration.[12]

PUBLIC RECORDS AS A TYPE OF RECORDS

If the concept of person is an appropriate criterion for dividing records and the notion of person as provenance is a suitable way of refining that criterion, it is now possible to approach the question of why public records are best considered a subspecies or type of records. Technically, public records could be considered a species of records, simply because the concept possesses all the attributes of records plus an additional one.[13] Here however, it is best considered a subspecies or type of records. There are two main reasons for this suggestion: the desirability of maintaining the systematic quality of the hierarchy of terms developed so far and the accidental nature of "public" as an attribute of records.

First of all, an asymmetry exists between the definitions of (a) information, documents, and records, and (b) public records. This asymmetry derives from the use of different classes of distinguishing attributes. While the definitions of information, documents, and records are all based on the notion of action, the definition of public records is based on that of the person who performs an action. This fact is not in itself enough to keep one from considering public records a species of records, should it be so desired. But it is both prudent and useful at this point to consider public records rather as a subspecies or type of records. After all, this study is intended as a point of departure, and a clear and simple map generally provides the best guide at the outset of any venture. Therefore, it seems best to retain the symmetry within the hierarchy of terms by pointing to the different relations existing between those terms when it comes time to divide records into public records. The different relations between those terms is economically brought out by considering public records a subspecies or type, not a species, of records. While perhaps risking the charge of pedantry, this tactical move offers some gain in clarity, simplicity, and potential for logical development.[14]

The second main reason for considering public records a subspecies or type of records lies in the accidental nature of *public* as an attribute of records. The quality of being public is logically accidental to the definition of records, in that it is neither part of the definition nor commensurate with it.[15] Records *may* be public or they may not—just as they may or may not be old, financial, or cartographic. A test of this "accidentalness" is whether it is reasonable to suppose that other species of documents may, like records, either be or not be public, no matter how the term may eventually be defined in full. Clearly, species of recorded information such as published books housed in a library could very well have a reasonable claim to being considered, in some way, public.

Despite the "accidentalness" of public as a quality of records, public records are nonetheless an acceptable subcategory or type of records for the purpose of division. As seen earlier, a generic notion of the person who makes or receives documents is inherent in the definition of records, and the notion of public falls within the general category of person. Moreover, within the present hierarchy of terms, the division of records into public records and other related subcategories must be based on a definition of the concept of person as the actor who makes or receives and preserves documents in the course of the conduct of affairs.

Since it has thus been determined that the logical bridge between records and public records is the concept of person—more specifically, the provenance-based concept of person as the only reasonable criterion for moving from records to public records through division of the species of records into its subspecies—the discussion may now move on to an analysis of the substantive meaning of "public records" within the framework so far developed.

NOTES

1. In speaking of "dividing" records, I am referring to what is generally called "logical division" or, more simply, "division." This activity differs technically from definition in that it involves splitting up a given category into its various subcategories, as opposed to determining the nature of a given species (or subcategory) by relating it to its genus (or superior category) by means of a differentiating attribute. Whether to speak of dividing records or defining public records, however, is largely a matter of perspective—which may readily be gained by reflecting briefly on the archival Tree of Porphyry set down in Figure 3 in Chapter 3. Since the entire archival hierarchy of terms may, from one perspective, be considered a form of logical division, it would be possible to speak here of *sub*dividing records into public records and whatever other subcategories may result. However, the neutral term "divide" has nonetheless been used in the present context. It might also be noted that division can further be distinguished from classification, by which a number of subcategories are brought together under a superior category. For a discussion of these matters, see Cohen and Nagel, *An Introduction to Logic*, pp. 241-44.

2. See pp. 63-65. While the elements of the definitions noted here were not explicitly set out above, a moment's reflection should demonstrate that these were, in fact, the elements distinguished. Peterson and Peterson provide a similar analysis of the elements of standard definitions in *Law*

(p. 12), though they do not treat the nature of the material and its form as separate elements.

The term *form*, it should be noted, is used here as loose shorthand for "physical form," itself an ambiguous term generally referring to the medium in which a record is embodied. The physical form of a record—electronic, video, paper, and so on—may be contrasted with (among other kinds of form) its functional form, such as correspondence, minutes, and reports. The latter seems traditionally to have been considered a secondary characteristic of records, following from both the manner in which a document was made or received and the purpose of that action. For some insight into the widespread ambiguity of the term *form*, see Bureau of Canadian Archivists, *Toward Descriptive Standards*, pp. 42-43. A useful beginning toward untangling some of this terminological confusion will be found in Duranti, "Diplomatics [Part I]," *Archivaria* 28, p. 15.

3. See Chapter 3, note 20.

4. See p. 62 above.

5. In one sense, of course, even the spoken word is "embodied" in the "physical form" of sound waves. However, the stipulation that, for present purposes, "physical form" refers to things such as floppy disks, photographic emulsions, and leaves of paper limits the notion of form to things stable enough for intelligence or information to be "recorded" on them.

6. *Funk & Wagnalls*, p. 1089.

7. At this point in the discussion, phrases such as "the public" are not intended to convey any substantive meaning. As yet, they are used in an attempt to determine only that the concept of person is the best criterion for delimiting the general kind of thing that "public" refers to—namely, a person or persons of *some* sort. It is to be hoped, therefore, that readers will, for the moment, hold in abeyance whatever substantial definition of "the public" they may bring to the discussion.

8. Schellenberg, *Modern Archives*, p. 16, emphasis added. T. R. Schellenberg, *The Management of Archives* (New York: Columbia University Press, 1965).

9. In archival terms, provenance may be defined as the entity (or actor or person) who makes or receives documents in the conduct of affairs and preserves them (Bellardo and Bellardo, *A Glossary for Archivists*, p. 27). From this concept and the concept of records, as noted in chapter 2, archivists derive the principle of provenance; namely, that the "records/archives of the same provenance must not be intermingled with those of any other provenance" (ibid.). Because of its obvious importance to this study, the concept of provenance will be examined more fully later on.

10. *Black's*, p. 1227. It should be noted, however, that "public *record*" is defined by the law in far narrower terms, echoing the long history of the term *record* discussed at the beginning of chapter 3 (ibid. p. 1231, emphasis

added). Provenance as "proceeding from" the public is here dubbed the "legal sense" of the term to distinguish this narrower meaning from the broader archival sense mentioned above—the latter being referred to simply as "provenance," considering the archival context of this study.

11. This need for consistency is an important aspect of any attempt at systematic investigation (see Cohen, *Reason and Nature*, pp. 106-14). It is even more so, perhaps, in a preliminary investigation of the sort attempted here—where the effort is toward providing a structure against which further studies may at least press, if not build upon.

12. All of this follows, as suggested, from the definition of records. Therefore, any disagreement with the qualifying notion of person presented here is actually a disagreement with the traditional definition of archives set out in the last chapter and assumed in this study for the sake of the argument. Anyone wishing to explore alternative definitions of records that limit or qualify the notion of person in a different way may find it useful to begin with such concepts as records proceeding from, relating to, affecting, open to, and belonging to the person known so far in the present study only as "the public."

13. Felber, *Terminology Manual*, p. 122.

14. It might also be noted that this move places the concept of records at the base of the hierarchy, underscoring it. This result is extremely useful if it is granted—as argued earlier in the sketch of archival theory—that the nature of records should provide a basis for any consideration of the nature of archival studies. Records, as the lowest species in the hierarchy, may therefore be considered the fundamental concept, the point of departure in any consideration of the nature of archival studies.

15. On logically accidental qualities, see Cohen and Nagel, *An Introduction to Logic*, pp. 237-38.

Chapter 5

Public Records

Given the general form of a definition of public records arrived at so far, which limits the notion of public to a kind of person who makes or receives and preserves documents, the substance of that definition must now be determined. What sort of person is this "public" by which the concept of records is to be qualified? As with the analysis of records, an examination of common definitions of the term provides a useful starting point.

THE PUBLIC IN COMMON AND LEGAL USAGE

Since this study is written within the context of a modern democratic polity, common language definitions and those drawn from standard legal sources will naturally reflect a democratic bias. This fact should prove a benefit rather than a liability, since it allows the discussion to begin with provisional definitions most likely to be readily understood and agreed on by the majority of readers. As works of analysis from Plato to recent linguistic philosophers attest, there is merit in beginning with the familiar. Plenty of time remains, after laying the appropriate groundwork, for attempts at universality.

In both common and legal usage, the public is an ambiguous entity closely related to another ambiguous entity called the people. The public is variously defined as "the people of a locality or nation," "the inhabitants of a state," and "the whole body politic, or the aggregate of the citizens of a state, nation, or municipality." The people is similarly defined not only as "the entire body of human beings living in the same country," but also as "the whole body of persons [in a state] invested with political rights; the enfranchised."[1]

As can be seen from these examples, *the public* and *the people* are ambiguous terms in that both refer to two distinct things: (1) the inhabitants of a state and (2) its citizens; in other words, the gross count of warm bodies and those involved by right in the governance of the state. This democratic distinction between inhabitants and citizens would be readily apparent in a state where citizenship was radically limited, for the enfranchised few who had a say in the governance of the state would be clearly visible against the backdrop of the many inhabitants who were merely governed. The enfranchised members of such a state (citizens, if you will), being inhabitants as well, would also be subject to the laws, although their involvement in making those laws, or at least empowering the legislators, would almost certainly set them apart as somehow privileged.

However, the situation is quite different in English-speaking countries today that enjoy a popular franchise, and this can make for no end of confusion. The basic complexities of democratic life arise largely from the fact that virtually all the inhabitants of such a state are, at the same time, its citizens.[2] As members of democratic states, we are both individual subjects who are ruled and citizens who collectively share in the ruling function. We wear two hats, and may at times find ourselves understandably confused about which is which as we try to untangle our purely private interests as subjects from our citizenly obligations as members of the sovereign tribunal, the collective source of political authority in the state.[3] Still, the distinction between citizens and inhabitants—or, more accurately, between citizens and *subjects*, considering the stress laid here on their relative positions within the state—remains as clear in a democracy as in a state with a far more limited franchise. It must be admitted, though, that the notions of the public and the people are understandably prone to a measure of ambiguity in a democratic polity.[4]

THE PUBLIC IN ARCHIVAL USAGE

In order to decide which of these two common notions of the public—as subjects and citizens—is to be preferred when defining public records for present purposes, it is first necessary to consider how they relate to the way that archivists view such records. Typically, archivists define public records as "government re-

cords," or "records accumulated by government agencies," thereby
equating the public with the government.[5] They generally go on,
in the traditional manner, to characterize the government as consisting of three organs or branches (depending on which organic
metaphor is preferred, the body or a tree) performing, or responsible for, three distinct functions: the legislature, the executive, and
the judiciary.[6] The definition is then further set off against what is
taken to be the antithesis of public records, namely, *private* records—both of which together are taken to constitute the entire
universe of records, as black is set off against nonblack or white.[7]

In thus defining public records as government records while
considering government as tripartite and setting private off against
public, archivists have essentially sided with the "sovereign citizens" notion of the public. However, they have apparently not
embraced all that this notion implies, because their equation of
public with government records omits an important distinction
inherent in the concept. The government is, in fact, just an instrument that the sovereign citizens employ in governing themselves.
It is a complex of institutions to which the citizens delegate—by
provisions within the same constitution by which they formally
bind themselves to one another as equal members of the sovereign
power—a specific measure of their authority.[8] Still, it is understandable that archivists, who in many cases work in bureaucratic
agencies, should tend to define the public as simply the government. The government may be only an instrument of the sovereign
citizens, but it is far more tangible. Unlike the sovereign per se, the
government can be found in charge of a payroll, housed in build-
ings, and possessed of myriad files.

PRIVATE RECORDS AND PAPERS

Just as archivists' definition of public records as government
records comes close to the "sovereign citizens" notion of the public,
their definition of private records as nongovernmental records
comes close to the "inhabitants of a state" or "subjects" notion of
the public. This symmetry is obvious if one considers that the
definition of private records is considered the *antithesis* of public
records. If government records are the records of the sovereign and
the dichotomy between the sovereign and the sovereign's subjects

includes all persons within a state, then all records that are *not* of the sovereign must be records of the sovereign's subjects.

The same symmetry between archivists' definitions of public and private records and the conceptions of the public as the sovereign and the sovereign's subjects holds true, though somewhat less obviously, even when one realizes that North American archivists have been in the habit of defining private records as those of nongovernmental "organizations and institutions."[9] The difficulty here is that, in limiting private records to those of organizations, archivists exclude the largest and most obvious group of the sovereign's subjects: individual persons.[10] However, North American archivists fill in this gap, completing the field which provides the symmetry sought for here, by contrasting private *records* with private or personal *papers*—by which natural accumulations of personal and family materials are distinguished from the natural accumulations of material deriving from organizations.[11]

This common archival distinction between private records and papers, however, is more a historical accident than a result of rational consideration and requires only brief consideration. The story of how North American archivists came to speak of the records of organizations and the papers of persons is long and involved. Essentially, though, it is a bow to those eighteenth- and nineteenth-century collectors of manuscripts and their descendants who, long before the emergence of archival repositories working from the European-based principles that still guide archival work, sought to salvage whatever material they could find that might prove of value for historical research. The often fragmentary material gathered from diverse sources and usually created by individual persons was generally arranged more in the manner of the artificial subject classifications used by librarians to deal with discrete items than according to archival principles respecting the organic unity of bodies of records—as perhaps befits such things as isolated autograph letters of famous persons.

Although such material still lies outside the province of what has been defined as records, early archivists, attempting to mark off their professional turf, failed to press the distinction between these miscellaneous collections and the organic bodies of records made or received in the course of affairs by persons and families. The archivists, as one commentator puts it, in effect "assumed that [all] manuscripts [whether or not they had archival qualities] were hopelessly lost to the librarians, and as part of their battle to prevent the same thing from happening to archives they emphasized the differences between historical manuscripts and archives."[12] Generally working with organic accumulations of records generated through the administration of the organizations that employed them, archivists set themselves apart from curators of manuscripts, making a verbal distinction between the records of organizations and the papers or manuscripts of persons and families, whether the latter possessed the distinguishing qualities of records or not. Clearly, this was a classic case of throwing out the baby with the bathwater—though the situation has largely, if not completely, been rectified.[13]

This analysis of common usage and archival terminology provides a prima facie case for equating the public with the sovereign, as contrasted with persons and organizations subject to the sovereign. Both everyday language and archival terminology, when freed from ambiguity and unnecessary distinctions, not only permit this interpretation but also support it. This is not to claim that such an interpretation needs no further support but that the analysis so far encourages further exploration. A useful method of supporting this interpretation is to expand on, refine, and test it within an archival context. Before doing so directly, however, it is necessary to address the critics and examine alternative models that now hold the field.

THE ILLUSORY PUBLIC AND PRIVATE BOUNDARY

The most ambitious criticism faced by the present study is not directed at the substantive interpretation so far offered. It is directed, rather, at the very attempt to distinguish public from private records. One commentator, for instance, argues that "the separation of the 'public' from the 'private'...is probably a record keeper's nightmare, and even a chimaera." This claim may be true in the limited sphere that was under consideration, a Minister of the Crown's right to claim that some portion of his records are not public but private.[14] It could be true, as the author comes close to insisting, that ministers forego any claim to privacy when they enter public life. This argument may or may not be true. What matters for present purposes is that the argument itself would be completely unintelligible if it did not take for granted a prior distinction between public and private. We take this argument seriously—consider it intelligible, that is—mainly because we assume, with the author, that things such as claims to *privacy* and *public* life really do exist, however those terms may be defined and whether or not the author's argument is accepted.

Another commentator, seeking to persuade archivists to focus their appraisals of the value of records and the acquisitions that result from them on broad areas transcending all distinctions about the nature of records creators, claims that institutions in the "public and private sectors" are today in fact *integrated,* which is tantamount to claiming that they have somehow melded into one.[15] The author's examples, however, refer only to the obvious fact that governments both hire private businesses to do certain jobs and set down guidelines for regulating them. Contractual delegation and regulations, as complicated a picture as they may result in, hardly argue in any persuasive way the actual *integration* of government and business. More important, the very notion of two distinguishable "sectors" assumes a distinction between public and private as the basis of an intelligible discussion—no matter how those terms may be defined, and whether or not the author's argument is accepted.

By far the freshest and most promising recent sketch, in archival terms, of how public and private affairs are "inextricably linked in myriad ways" will be found in Terry Eastwood's "Reflections on the Development of Archives in Canada and Australia."[16] Unfortunately, though, at one point the author's unobjectionable exaggeration about "the illusory public and private boundary" would, if taken at face value, logically undermine his otherwise persuasive account of archives' and archivists' responsibility toward what he calls the ideal of democratic accountability and cultural continuity in a democratic polity. For his entire construction rests on a strong, if largely tacit, commitment to a prior distinction between the public and private realms.

A certain tendency to diminish and blur the distinction between public and private may be justly described as rhetorical exaggeration, however legitimate in context. Still, that characterization by no means suggests that in *some* ways the distinction between public and private may not only be illusory but retrograde. At the very least, any such distinction seems very much illusory when it is a question, say, of how to arrange and describe records. The public

-private distinction is subsidiary to the definition of records, which inevitably means that all *records*—like all nonarchival documents—must be treated in the same manner in all cases (such as that of arrangement and description) where the only question at issue is their existence as (their possession of the nature of) records. In other words, whether the material at hand consists of records or nonarchival documents, in principle it should be described according to the same method, however extensive it may be or whatever its provenance.[17]

JENKINSON ON PUBLIC, SEMIPUBLIC, AND PRIVATE RECORDS

Assuming that general criticism of the distinction between public and private may be largely ignored for present purposes, alternative models of public and private records that now hold the field require examination. Although many commentators have touched on these concepts to some degree in passing, there has really been only one sustained effort in the English-speaking world influential enough to warrant detailed scrutiny. It is found in the classification of English archives developed primarily by Jenkinson.[18]

Though much might be said about the classification as a whole, the main area of interest for this study is the division of records into what Jenkinson calls public, semipublic, and private. In this scheme, public records, as in North America, consist largely of government records within all jurisdictions and at all levels. Private records, on the other hand, include "the documentary results of every kind of Undertaking or Jurisdiction conducted for private advantage or satisfaction, whether by an Individual or by a Corporation or Institution."[19] In other words, the seeking of a particular sort of "advantage or satisfaction" is judged the criterion that distinguishes private persons from the public. By parity of reasoning, it must be assumed that Jenkinson means to speak of public records as those resulting from affairs undertaken for *public* "advantage or satisfaction" or, as is commonly said, in the public interest.

Without doubting for a moment that private interests may be distinguished from public, it must be noted that there is a difficulty with thus attempting to distinguish the public from private persons according to their interests or aims. This difficulty is clearly demonstrated by the major position held by semipublic records in Jenkinson's classification. Semipublic bodies, he says, are those "which, existing primarily for private advantage or satisfaction, usually discharge more or less Public functions and are privileged and controlled accordingly," such as banks, insurance companies, educational institutions, charities, and professional bodies.[20] The difficulty here is not that Jenkinson locates a grey area between private persons and the public; in a complex world, there will always be an area in which fundamental distinctions have to be qualified. The difficulty is that Jenkinson seems in some ways too much a pragmatist to tolerate for long the tension between public and private and settles for a less than satisfactory characterization of what pragmatic compromise often speaks of, in an appeal to reason and moderation, as "the middle ground."[21]

A symptom of this difficulty lies in the very size and prominence of this supposed middle ground. Offered as a category unto itself, semipublic provides no principled way of distinguishing between public and private persons, because its very existence as a formal category precludes any possible resolution of difficult cases into the contrasting categories of public and private. The difficulty becomes evident when his construction is examined more closely. One notices, first, that Jenkinson is not really speaking of semipublic bodies at all—at least if *semi* is taken to mean something genuinely halfway between two extremes, a blending of both, as grey is halfway between white and black. What he speaks of are organizations that are, in his terms, *both* public and private. Though private by intention, he assumes, they are both public *and* private in their effects—in the interests they actually serve. In other words, they constitute something less like grey than like a black and white checkerboard, not so much a blend of extremes as an unmixed combination of both.

The distinction between intentions and effects is made here only for the purpose of clarifying Jenkinson's exposition of semipublic bodies. In his scheme, private effects follow directly from private intentions, whereas public effects follow inadvertently. It might also be noted that public effects, in Jenkinson's scheme and according to the distinctions worked out earlier, are effects upon the public as the sovereign's subjects or the whole of the inhabitants of a state. This may seem confusing in light of the preliminary judgment offered above that the noun *public* is best reserved for speaking about the sovereign rather than the sovereign's subjects. The confusion, however, is only verbal, since the sovereign's main concern, by definition, is to rule the *whole* of its subjects. Effects upon the public as the whole of the inhabitants of a state are *public* effects because, affecting the whole, they are the legitimate business of the public as sovereign. Private effects, by contrast, are those that affect individual subjects or particular groups of them, rather than the whole.

One also notices, after his special use of the term *semi*, that Jenkinson rather too quickly assumes that semipublic bodies may be characterized as having only private intentions and both private and public effects. Some of these bodies, of which voluntary civic and charitable organizations perhaps come most readily to mind, can hardly be thought of as having anything but *public* intentions. Modern civil liberties organizations, for example, are generally founded with the broad intent of ensuring that the government of the day is continually reminded of its obligation to uphold consti-tutional provisions regarding the basic rights of citizens (such as freedom of speech) and of subjects (such as due process of law). Clearly, the intent of such organizations is to promote the public interest.[22] The *effects* of their work, however, are both public (by intention) and private (inadvertently). By capturing the ear of the sovereign's government on issues that deal with all citizens or all subjects of the sovereign, their work has obvious public effects. Indeed, the monetary contributions that such organizations may from time to time receive from agencies of the sovereign only reinforce the claim that they have public effects, and perhaps lend credence to their more particular claim to represent at least a portion of "the institutionalization of civic conscience," however unofficial.[23] But when they go to court to assist an individual subject on, say, a question of due process, they not only produce a public effect by drawing attention to a matter of *general* interest (and perhaps even change a given law or policy). They also pro-duce an inadvertent private effect by assisting that individual subject. To whatever degree the test case may be generalized, it is also a single case affecting the life of a particular subject at a particular moment in time.[24] Jenkinson does not take into account these variations on the relations between the public and private intentions and effects of certain organizations falling within the category he calls semipublic.

Several conclusions can be drawn from this examination of Jenkinson's depiction of semipublic bodies. For one thing, if some semipublic bodies have both public intentions and effects, then it cannot follow that semipublic bodies are, as Jenkinson defines them, those that exist primarily for private advantage or satisfaction while having public effects as well. His characterization is simply not broad enough to encompass the actual traits of bodies offered as exemplifying the category. Moreover, because the category of semipublic bodies includes both organizations that have private intentions and organizations that have public intentions, such bodies cannot be defined solely by the intentions underlying them. The intentions of different organizations within the same category point in opposite directions, possessing nothing in common, and thereby tear the category apart.

However, since both kinds of organization have both public and private *effects*, whether intended or inadvertent, the category might still seem capable of being salvaged, should Jenkinson abandon "interest" for "effect" as the distinguishing mark of semipublic bodies. Among semipublic bodies would have to be included all those having both public and private effects, independent of whether those effects are intended or inadvertent, because organizations with both sorts of effect have been included in the category. However, this combination of both sorts of organization within the same category returns us to the first objection to the category of semipublic bodies: it is not so much a blending of public and private as an acceptance of both existing side by side, independent of each other and incapable of resolving difficult cases because no meaningful link exists between two superficially complementary solitudes.

Given these considerations, it must be admitted that Jenkinson's notion of a kind of organization halfway between public and private aids the present discussion largely in a negative way, since it leads toward a conceptual dead end. It does so for two main reasons. First, as a category, semipublic fails to throw any light on the distinction between public and private records creators, serving more as a pragmatic dumping ground for a disparate group of records creators that appear to possess characteristics of both public and private bodies, distinguished from one another on the basis of the interests they serve. Second, the notion of interests as the distinguishing mark between public and private organizations cannot be applied consistently.

However, this notion of semipublic bodies is nonetheless instructive. Jenkinson was attempting to develop a classification that would do justice not only to records resulting from the conduct of contemporary affairs but also to records generated in England over the past 800 years or so. He clearly recognized that some series of records—those resulting from the exercise of particular functions—had at various times been generated by different kinds of records creator. This recognition means that a theoretical classification scheme drawn up today will almost certainly require cross-references from one category to another, in order to do justice to historical reality—at least if one is determined (as Jenkinson was) to attempt to relate a single series of records to a single class of records creator over time.[25] Unfortunately, he chose to distinguish records creators by the criterion of "interests," which does not work well.

All the same, Jenkinson points us in the right direction by showing that the distinction between public and private records creators should be capable of dealing with potential shifts of records creators from one category to the other over time. Jenkinson's historical sensitivity may have emerged within the context of developing a classification scheme for England's 800 years' worth of records, which would not seem to apply to the North American experience, and the classification is based on the notion of the "interests" of records creators, which does not work. But he nonetheless reminds us that good theory should be as broad as possible, pressing ever toward universal validity. The distinction between public and private records creators, like the definition of records, will take us beyond parochialism only to the extent that it can be applied to other societies today and over time.

Although developed within the context of "ancient" English records and in an attempt to distinguish public from private records creators on the basis of interest, the historical sensitivity displayed by Jenkinson is dependent on neither. There are two reasons for this. First, the temporal extent of English records and the accompanying changes in the public or private nature of records creators only seems nonapplicable to "modern" records in North America when one forgets the increasing sphere of public jurisdiction since the rise of the welfare state. Even a parochial account of the nature of public and private records creators within recent North American experience will remain unpersuasive unless it displays some amount of sensitivity to historical change. Second, given that such changes in the public and private character of records creators do in fact occur, *any* criterion used to distinguish between the two—"interest" or any other— is necessarily bound to, or dependent on, the prior fact of change. In other words, shifts between the public and private nature of the creator of a certain series of records may be *described* with greater precision by employing a particular criterion for distinguishing between the two. That description will be better or worse depending on the criterion chosen. However, the description of the fact—not its *explanation*— can but follow the existence of the fact itself.

THE PRINCIPLE OF PROVENANCE

Holding in mind for a moment the broader ground toward which Jenkinson's historical considerations press the discussion, it will be useful to take a brief step backward and note that what is sought has not yet been found: a workable criterion for distinguishing between public and private records creators. Jenkinson's criterion of "interest," which may seem the most promising contender on intuitive grounds, has obviously not provided the solid base that is sought.[26] In fact, this or any similar criterion begs the question, since it does not tell us how public and private persons are to be distinguished; it only removes the question a step further from immediacy. If, for example, it is claimed that public records creators are to be distinguished from private ones because they serve the public interest, it still remains necessary to determine how to distinguish the public, with its interests, from private records creators, with their presumably divergent interests. If it is already agreed, say, that the public is best considered as the sovereign and private persons as the sovereign's subjects (whether singly or in groups) then well and good. One may *then* go on to describe the nature of the public interest accordingly, should one care to attempt it. But any account of the nature of that interest would depend on the definition of the public already provided.

To say this is to reiterate from another angle a point stressed in the previous chapter: however much it may be pressed against, intuitively or otherwise, the definition of public records is bound by the notion of provenance. It follows that anything other than a direct account of the nature of the public as a records-creating person offers at best circumlocution and perhaps even invites confusion.[27] Accordingly, since at least the outline of a direct account has already been provided—framed as a distinction (understood in modern democratic polities) between the public as the sovereign citizens and the private realm of those subject to the sovereign, individually or in groups—the rest of the discussion may most profitably be spent in expanding on, refining, and testing that account within an archival context.

In order to move the discussion forward, it will be useful to review the definition of public records to which the interpretation so far leads. As noted, the concept of the public as sovereign provides a substantive account of the notion of person, which is fundamental to the definition of public records. Slotting this concept into the appropriate place in the definition of records leads to a definition of public records as "documents made or received in the conduct of affairs and preserved *by the sovereign*." By contrast, the coordinate definition of private records fills in the person blank—the last phrase—with "by the sovereign's subjects."

Although clearly not enough in itself to provide as sharp an analytical tool as one would like, this definition of public records at least has the merit of offering a substantive notion of the public. Some definitions do not. Consider, for example, the definition of public records offered by theorists of diplomatics. "*A document is public*," from this perspective, "*if it is created by a public person or by his command or in his name*, that is, if the will determining the creation of the document is public in nature."[28] Fair enough. But what, exactly, is a public person with its public will? The response, essentially, is that a public person is "a juridical person performing functions *considered to be public by the juridical system in which the person acts*."[29] In other words, the public must be considered as whatever it is considered as in any society at any time.

For archival theory, this example from a kindred discipline offers both insight and danger. Not only does it suggest that the definition of public records will venture beyond parochialism only to the extent that it can be applied universally—a position toward which Jenkinson's historical sensitivity also leads. It also suggests that a realistic account of the public must come to grips with the notions of authorized and delegated action.

The example presents danger in that it tends toward a somewhat abstract level of theory. Diplomatists rightly suggest that the definition of public records should aim at universality and different juridical systems will tend to characterize the public in different ways. However, by not defining that concept substantively, they would seem to have passed by the opportunity to gain a clear view of what remains constant about public persons from polity to polity and, by implication, what aspects of the concept undergo change. One can only hope that the example is not unfair or in some other way inappropriate; after all, any concept with potentially universal application would suffice. However, the diplomatic treatment of public persons strikes me in somewhat the same way as would the suggestion that beautiful persons are best considered as those persons considered beautiful in any given society. While not hesitating to agree, and perhaps welcoming the implication that different societies will have different notions of beauty, one might nonetheless wonder exactly what concept the word *beautiful* is meant to indicate.[30] This danger having been skirted, the insight offered by diplomatic theory will have to be applied before too long.

However, as useful as it may be to provide a substantive definition of the public, the archival definition of public records arrived at so far can be improved on. To do so effectively requires a second look at the nature of provenance, which lies at the heart of a "person-centered" definition of public records.[31] First, though, a word of warning. The overall effectiveness of this approach requires the establishment of several related concepts, none of which may at first seem to bear directly on the question of the nature of public records. Only after agreement is reached on the general relevance of these concepts will it be possible to apply them directly to the question at issue.

Provenance is generally defined by archivists as the entity who makes or receives documents in the conduct of affairs and preserves them.[32] Literally meaning origin or source, provenance is open to a measure of ambiguity, even among archivists, because there are various "sources" of the records they deal with, depending on how the term is defined.[33] Clarity therefore requires a brief attempt at contrasting standard archival usage with other related ways of using the term *provenance*. At least three senses of provenance as the source of records can be distinguished from standard archival usage. The first is what might be called custodial provenance: the entity or entities who maintained a particular body of records over time. The second is what might be called transmissive provenance: the entity from whom a particular body of records was received into custody by an archival repository.[34] The third is what might be called diplomatic provenance: the entity who actually authored the records.[35]

All or none of these types of provenance may coincide with archival provenance. Imagine, for instance, a government with separate departments of education, archives, and records management, the latter maintaining a central records center for the whole government. All three may be considered independent records creators. Within the department of education, a senior official sends a memorandum to the head of administration. The memorandum is read, acted on, and filed for reference. Maintained over time by the department, it is eventually transferred by an administrative officer to the department of archives as part of a series of memoranda dealing with office policy and procedure.[36] In this case, the department of education made *and* received the document in the conduct of affairs (archival provenance), authored it (diplomatic provenance), maintained custody of it over time (custodial provenance), and transferred it to the department of archives (transmissive provenance).

Imagine, on the other hand, a letter received by the same senior official from the attorney general's department. It is read, acted on, filed, and later sent to the department of records management for storage in the records center. After a number of years, it is sent from the records center to the department of archives. In this case, the attorney general's department authored the document (diplomatic provenance), the department of education received it in the conduct of affairs (archival provenance), the department of records management maintained custody of it over time and transferred it to the department of archives (custodial and transmissive provenance).

Several points may be noted from these examples. For one thing, custodial provenance refers primarily to physical rather than legal custody. Presumably, the department of education had every right to recall the document, or the series of which it formed a part, from the department of records management at any time. It follows, moreover, that to speak of archival provenance as documents made or received *and preserved* by a particular entity implies that the word *preservation* is used in the legal rather than the physical sense of "maintenance over time." With respect to archival provenance, the notion of creation refers only to original documents that are directed internally and reference copies of documents that are sent outward from an agency. A carbon copy of the letter authored by the attorney general's department and filed therein would have the archival provenance of that department, whereas the original sent to the department of education has the archival provenance of the latter.

PROVENANCE AND FUNCTION

Over the years, this equation of archival provenance with the physical or juridical person who makes or receives documents in the conduct of affairs and preserves them has stood archivists in good stead. Not all archivists would, of course, agree. One commentator, for example, suggests that archival provenance should be redefined to include custodial and transmissive (but not diplomatic) provenance. The reasoning behind this recommendation seems sound. The more knowledge archivists have about these several kinds of provenance, the better they will understand the overall historical and administrative context of the records under their care and, in applying that understanding, the better the care they will be able to provide.[37] Nonetheless, it seems reasonable to believe that this need for as much contextual knowledge as possible can be stressed while maintaining a clear sense of the kind of provenance that is distinctly archival. As discussed earlier, distinctions provide clarity; they do not necessarily imply divorce.

However well this concept of provenance has served archivists by and large, there is at least one aspect of this equation that has not often been noted. What exactly is meant by the phrase "in the conduct of affairs"? In the traditional definition of archives, this phrase is inextricably tied to the person who makes or receives and preserves documents. "In the conduct of affairs" serves to help define that person, pointing toward the larger sphere of activity to which the actions of making or receiving and preserving documents contribute. For archival purposes, persons are to a large extent characterized by the kinds of activities they are involved in, activities in which records are generated as a matter of course. In other words, if it is true that an adequate definition of public records must focus on the concept of person, it is equally true that, for archivists, persons must be characterized largely by the particular areas of activity in which they make or receive and preserve documents.[38]

For convenience, these spheres or areas of activity will from here on be referred to as functions. Though often hard to pin down, the term is widely used by archivists.[39] It would doubtless be useful to consider at length the relations among such concepts as action, activity, sphere of activity, function, and mandate. Here it is necessary only to note that creation, receipt, and preservation of documents are specific kinds of action that form part of one or more larger wholes and that these wholes may be considered as such because they draw all the parts together toward a common end.

These wholes may be of different sizes. One may speak, for example, of the function of acquisition within an archival agency and note that the documents variously comprising contact files and the accessions register are all created and preserved in the course of exercising that function. By the same token, one might speak more broadly of the function of the archival agency within its larger administrative context. In this latter case, acquisition (along with appraisal, arrangement, description, and so on) would represent but a single part—perhaps a subfunction—of the larger function of, say, preserving (and, by implication, communicating) records. That these functions, at whatever level, are comprised of actions directed toward a common end seems an acceptable (albeit undemonstrated) assumption for present purposes, in that archivists generally speak as though words such as *acquisition* and, more broadly, *preservation* have some intelligible meaning. Since their generality implies that such terms cannot in themselves refer to discrete actions, they must represent a kind of shorthand for composite series of actions. Since archivists seem to refer to goals when using such terms, pointing toward jobs to be done, it follows that these general words are commonly considered end-directed.[40]

Given the traditional definition of archives (or records), "in the conduct of affairs" thus provides a kind of shorthand. Archival provenance, as assumed by the traditional definition, means more than simply the entity who makes or receives and preserves documents. It also binds that entity to the function it performs while generating (making, receiving, preserving) such documents. Accordingly, the definition of public records can be further refined as "documents made or received and preserved when performing its function or functions by the sovereign." Here, however, it has been noted only that a function of *some* sort is involved. Since it has tentatively been determined that the person who generates public records is the sovereign, the function that the sovereign performs must also be specified—just as, after it had been determined that a person of some sort generates public records, a substantive definition of that person had to be provided.

PROVENANCE AND LEGITIMACY

Before taking this further step, however, it should be noted that "in the conduct of affairs" does more than simply point to the function performed by records creators. Perhaps it would be more suitable to say that the notion of function embedded within this pregnant phrase implies more than at first appears. Clearly, to speak about, say, the function of acquisition performed by an archival repository is not only to speak about an area or sphere of activity. It is to assume, as well, that such a repository is, in fact, the agency *entitled* to perform that function, the agency that acquires material in the conduct of its authorized or legitimate affairs.

For archivists, diplomatics probably provides the most familiar way of characterizing the cluster of ideas involving entitlement, authority, and legitimacy. Theorists of this discipline link the ideas of person and function through the notion of competence, defined as "the authority and capacity of carrying out a determined sphere of activities within one function, attributed to a given office or an individual." Because of its familiarity and precision, this definition provides a useful way of delimiting the notion of legitimacy as it relates to provenance. However, since I have been using the term *function* in a broader way, for consistency's sake the phrase "carrying out a determined sphere of activities within one function" should be read as "carrying out a function."[41]

This concept of competence or legitimacy is hardly an innovation. It was assumed not only in the example of an archival acquisition program but also in those relating to the departments of archives, records management, education, and attorney general. A further example, verging on absurdity, will demonstrate how closely we connect the exercise of a function with the legitimate or competent exercise of it. Imagine, for instance, a state archives with separate divisions responsible for acquisition, reference, and administration. The reference manager conceives the notion that, to serve its clients better, the institution needs to somehow "purify" its program for the acquisition of public records—and that this change has to be made immediately by whatever means possible. For reasons not entirely clear, he draws up a new acquisition policy himself, signs it in his capacity as reference manager, and circulates it to all government departments. Given this admittedly unlikely situation, do we consider the resulting document in exactly the same light as the preexisting acquisition policy generated while performing his function by the acquisition manager? Obviously not, because we take for granted the union between exercising a function and exercising it legitimately or competently. That is how we expect things to operate in the normal course of the conduct of affairs. The word *normal* tacitly qualifies the terms *course* or *conduct* in the traditional definition of archives, with the implied *norms* deriving from the system of authority in which those affairs take place. In the present example, the reference manager has exercised an aspect of the acquisition function without authority—noncompetently.

For present purposes, the most important question raised by this example concerns the document's provenance. What is the provenance of the copy of this acquisition policy that arrives in, say, the department of education? The archival provenance, as with any other document received by the department in the course of its affairs, is clearly the department itself, which has the competence to receive such documents. But what about the provenance of the copy filed centrally in the archives? It was certainly *received* in the legitimate conduct of affairs by the filing unit in the administration division, because one aspect of that division's function (let us assume) is to provide for the reception and custody of internal documents and reference copies of those sent outward. It would also be *made* in the legitimate conduct of affairs if it had been authored by the acquisition manager, who is the officer competent to issue such documents. However, since it was made without authority by the reference manager, determining its provenance becomes problematic.

This situation can be clarified by drawing on the diplomatic notion of authenticity, a concept related to competence. Diplomatically, authentic documents are those "written according to the practice of the time and place indicated in the text, and signed with the name(s) of the person(s) competent to create them."[42] Accordingly, the document must be considered inauthentic, since the problematic aspect of the reference manager's acquisition policy has to do mainly with its noncompetent authorship. But how does this translate into terms of archival provenance? Note, in this regard, that the copy of the document received by the education department, despite its regular provenance, would also be diplomatically inauthentic, because such status derives from the quality of its authorship, which remains the same no matter who received the document in whatever context. As a result, a document's diplomatic authenticity or inauthenticity does not necessarily correspond to the regularity or irregularity of its archival provenance. In other words, archival and diplomatic provenance are not identical. However, in cases such as the present one, where authorship is the determining factor regarding the status of the creation aspect of archival provenance, the notions of provenancial regularity and diplomatic authenticity do coincide.

Given these considerations, at least two ways of characterizing documents of irregular provenance emerge. One possibility would be to consider them archivally inauthentic. This would involve adapting the terminology of diplomatics and applying it to archival provenance, not only in cases involving irregular authorship, but also in all cases of documents noncompetently made or received. In the present case, the copy of the reference manager's acquisition policy filed in the archives could be said to have been noncompetently made in the course of the reference division's affairs, having the inauthentic provenance of that division with regard to its creation.

The other possibility would be to consider provenancially inauthentic documents nonrecords. All documents illegitimately (or noncompetently) made or received in the course of exercising a function would be archivally null and void. Though somewhat extreme, this second possibility at least has the merit of emphasizing the importance of provenance to the archival concept of records, implying that irregular provenance is not provenance at all. If the concept of function is essential to the notion of archival provenance and function is wedded to the universal concept of competence or legitimacy, then it could be argued that any document made at any time or place can *have* archival provenance only if it is made or received and preserved in the legitimate exercise of any given function. Accordingly, on this argument, since the archival definition of records is bound to the notion of provenance, documents made or received illegitimately or noncompetently would not be records in the archival sense. Archivally, they would be nonrecords, without status—nullities. They would still be *documents*, in the sense of recorded information, because even instruments generated by unauthorized persons set down an intelligible message capable of later recall. But they would not be records. While usefully emphasizing the necessary relation between competence and provenance, this argument none the less goes a step too far. The definition of records requires only that documents have an archival provenance of some sort, specifying nothing about the quality of that provenance. Therefore, no warrant exists for dubbing documents of irregular provenance nonrecords.[43]

My own preference in the present context is to adapt the diplomatic notion of authenticity. This concept not only retains the strong link between the archival notions of provenance and records offered by the concept of nonrecords but also provides a substantive term for distinguishing the provenancial status of records. The danger of confusion between the diplomatic and archival use of the term *authentic* inevitably arises, but that danger arises with any careful use of terms, as with the different kinds of provenance discussed earlier. Forging another link between archival studies and diplomatics, while carefully distinguishing related concepts where necessary can, in fact, only strengthen the development of archivists' conceptual tools.

In the present case, for example, adapting the notion of authenticity invites consideration of the related diplomatic notion of a genuine document, defined as one which "is truly what it purports to be," namely, one that is not "forged, counterfeit, or [has not been] somehow tampered with at some time."[44] This distinction between authenticity and genuineness makes it possible to refine the notion of archival authenticity by excluding the quality of genuineness or falsity from any determination of provenance. The copy of the reference manager's acquisition policy received by the education department would have been provenancially authentic but false if it had borne the forged signature of the acquisition manager, although the provenance would be the acquisition rather than the

reference division. The copy filed in the archives would likewise
be false, but would have the authentic provenance of the acquisition division.[45] Despite the useful distinctions that can be made,
this adaptation of diplomatic usage does not change the fundamental point at issue here, whatever terms are employed. Legitimacy
(or competence), like function, is integral to the concept of provenance.

PROVENANCE AND AGENCY

This analysis of archival provenance has so far teased out the
elements of function and legitimacy. Before turning to a direct
application of the analysis to the concept of public records, one
further element of provenance requires brief mention. It will be
recalled that diplomatists speak not only of documents created by
a person, but also of those created "by his command or in his
name."[46] Employed here is the concept of delegation or agency.
This notion has been defined as the "relation in which one person
acts for or represents another by [the] latter's authority."[47] Like
competence or legitimacy, this concept has been assumed throughout the discussion so far. It is, in fact, but one area in which the
broader concept of legitimacy can be witnessed in action.

For the sake of exposition, consider the concept of agency within
a modern democratic context. Among other things, it is difficult to
even think of the modern democratic sovereign without some
notion of this relationship of delegated authority. "The people" (in
this sense) are rarely seen to act, except through the representatives
of their own ultimate authority. One of these agents of the sovereign—the government—is often confused with the sovereign itself,
for the very reason that it gives to this apparently airy nothing a
local habitation and a name. However, what is loosely called "the
government"—generally referring only to the most obvious manifestations of the legislature, executive, and judiciary—is itself a
complex institution comprised of many organizational units performing a wide variety of functions. Administrations, authorities,
boards, bureaus, commissions, departments, and services may all
be counted among their number.[48] Though existing at different
degrees of delegation from the ultimate source of authority they all
partake of some portion of that authority and may therefore be
considered agents of the sovereign in their own right.[49]

The generic archival term for all such departments, boards, commissions, and so on—agencies—is thus entirely apt.[50] Just as the term *agent* typically (and historically) refers to a physical person acting for another (or a juridical person in the form of a position; "the chief archivist," as opposed to any given incumbent), the cognate term *agency* may reasonably be ascribed to a juridical person in the form of an "organization" acting for another. Accordingly, *agency* is the term that will be used from here on to refer to a juridical person (in the form of an organization) acting on behalf of the sovereign.

The logic of delegation from the sovereign authority can be taken one step further. In fact, one may include among such public bodies or agencies all schools, colleges, universities, hospitals, and corporations that ultimately derive their mandate (and usually a major share of their funding) from the sovereign — generally through the intermediate authority of the legislature or executive. All such agencies, because of the circumstances of their creation and continuing existence, are ultimately accountable to the sovereign. The logic of delegation (as the concept is used here) also extends to contractors hired by any such agency to produce goods or perform services on behalf of the agency, because they are themselves (at least under the terms of the contract) a species of agent.[51]

The same principle of agency through delegation can be applied to public officials at all levels. *Officials* may not be the best term to use, since the word is often applied only to those persons holding elected office, as distinguished from appointees, employees, and so on. From the perspective of this study, however, public officials may reasonably refer to all persons involved in making or receiving documents while performing the function or functions of an agency or office deriving its ultimate authority from the sovereign. That there are differences between heads of state and temporary data-entry clerks or contract archivists goes without saying. Still, the principle of agency can be applied to them all, regardless of position, since all of them are involved in conducting some aspect of the sovereign's legitimate business, at whatever level of delegation.[52]

The notion of agency thus broadens and refines the concept of archival provenance by extending the notion of person. It depends for its validity on the broad concept of competence, since agents can only legitimately be such if the persons for whom they act not only have the authority to delegate but also exercise that authority while performing their legitimate functions. As with the concepts of function and legitimacy, that of agency has its own place in the definition of public records, which may now be restated as follows: "documents made or received and preserved in the (legitimate) conduct of its function or functions by the sovereign *or its agents.*"[53]

THE FUNCTION OF THE SOVEREIGN

The notion of archival provenance based on the concept of person incorporates the notions of function, legitimacy, and agency. The first step toward applying these concepts fully to the concept of public records will be to determine the particular function that the sovereign performs in any given society. The public having been tentatively equated with the sovereign, that substantive definition must now be deepened and its universal applicability demonstrated.

Though allowing a measure of my own beliefs about the nature of sovereignty in a democratic polity to shape the earlier discussion about subjects, citizens, and their relation to "the people," I do not want to claim that this particular concept can be transported wholesale across the reaches of time and space.[54] It can be claimed, however, that the *function* performed by the sovereign citizens in a democracy today exists in virtually all societies. If such a function exists, the term *public* may reasonably be applied to whatever person, physical or juridical, exercises that function in a given society, since that person will be theoretically equivalent to the public as the sovereign citizens in a democratic polity. In other words, while our own concept of the public as members of modern democratic polities may not be universally applicable, the same term may be applied to all persons or institutions that perform the same function in other societies. The term is our own; the function is universal.

The basic function performed by the democratic sovereign comprised of all citizens is governance. Government of the people (as subjects), by the people (as citizens), for the people (as citizens) may be a complex and at times confusing business in a democracy, but the same function is found in all societies. However they may be characterized in any given society, rulers and ruled are a given and basic component of the human scene. More precisely, it can be said that "every society has a political system and...the function of every political system is the maintenance of a social order within a territorial framework by the exercise of authority."[55]

On this account, it may be said that the sovereign is the first and final authority in any given political system: the first, as the source from which all lesser authority derives by delegation; the final, as the last source of appeal against the actions and judgments of all lesser authorities.[56] The key word here is *authority*, which differs from *power* because of its legitimacy. As one commentator puts it, "authority is the right to command, and correlatively, the right to be obeyed. It must be distinguished from power, which is the ability to compel compliance, either through the use or the threat of force."[57] Put another way, authority represents the legitimate exercise of power.

There would seem to be several constant elements of such sovereign authority in all polities. Among them may be included the number of physical persons of which the sovereign is comprised, the means by which sovereignty was obtained, the reasons by which it is justified, and the interests that the sovereign serves. Sovereignty, as a result, may take on any number of forms, depending on how a given polity views these several elements. The manner in which the elements are arrayed matters little, however, so long as the authority of the sovereign—of the juridical person who performs the ruling function—is in fact *recognized* as such, its privileged position accepted as legitimate.[58]

The number of physical persons comprising the sovereign does not really matter, because the function of legitimate governance (of authority) remains intact whether the sovereign is deemed one person, a group, or the whole. The king in a monarchy, the party in an oligarchy, and the people in a democracy can all be legitimate forms of sovereignty. The means by which that sovereignty was obtained does not really matter, because the function of legitimate governance remains intact whether king, party, or people attained it by conquest, revolution, hereditary endowment, or common consent—at least where such methods of acquisition are recognized as legitimate. The means by which that sovereignty is justified does not really matter, because the function of legitimate governance remains intact (when recognized) whether a hereditary king appeals to God or the leaders of a successful people's revolution appeal to the law of nature. The interests that the sovereign serves do not really matter, because the function of legitimate governance remains intact (when recognized) whether the people as citizens rule themselves as subjects for the common good of all or the king rules the people as subjects for his own gain.[59] All these possibilities demonstrate the variety of forms that sovereignty may take. But what concerns the present inquiry primarily is the basic quality common to them all: legitimate governance, recognized as such.[60]

If it is accepted that this broad notion of sovereignty presents a reasonable approach to defining the public, then the definition of public records may be restated as follows: "all documents made or received and preserved in the conduct of *governance* by the sovereign or its agents."[61]

APPLYING THE CONCEPT OF PUBLIC RECORDS

While drawing together many of the concepts discussed so far, the definition of public records arrived at above cannot yet stand alone as a distillation of the present chapter, let alone the entire study. The definition may be logical, given the analysis of provenance. It may be reasonable, given the need for a substantive definition of the person who makes or receives and preserves public records. But it cannot stand alone, because its theoretical and practical utility have yet to be demonstrated. How much faith can ultimately be placed in logic and reason if their products are seen as *irrelevant* to those who may consider employing them?

I must confess to being of two minds about this procedure. On the one hand, I am loathe to sully my logical constructions with reference to mere concrete reality. On the other hand, I have spent more hours than I would care to admit studying theoretical works which, while to a certain extent logical and persuasive, have failed to *convince* because of their almost perverse refusal to deal with concrete reality. If the latter position is sided with for now, it is because I suspect that the former assumes a false distinction between the theoretical and the concrete, mistaking the concrete for the empirical. The theoretical and empirical may be distinct though complementary approaches to any subject, but theory can usefully be placed along a continuum from the abstract to the concrete, depending on various factors ranging from its own internal necessity to the author's respect for his readers.

With that caveat in mind, the remainder of the discussion will accordingly attempt to determine, from the concepts developed so far, the differences between public and private records within a number of typical situations. As these situations are explored, it will be useful to bear in mind a corollary of the analysis so far: public and private records are mutually exclusive categories. Records can be either public or private, but not both at the same time; semipublic and semiprivate are nonexistent categories of records. This is because no records creator can be both public and private at the same time. No records creator can be both public and private at the same time because records can only be generated through particular actions serving specific functions. Records can only be generated through particular actions serving specific functions because only one action can be done at a time and such actions cannot be ambiguous in the present context—cannot point in two directions, serving two opposed functions, at the same time.

Only one such unambiguous action can be done at a time because of the nature of the governing function that results in public records. The nature of the governing or ruling function is such that a person cannot both rule and be ruled at the same time.[62] This proposition follows from the previous discussion. If, as suggested, to rule is to have the right to command and, correlatively, the right to be obeyed, to *be* ruled is to have the obligation to accept command and, correlatively, the obligation to obey.[63] The right of the ruler can only exist as such in relation to the obligation of the ruled. Rights and obligations exist as opposite but necessary and complementary aspects of the same phenomenon. It is difficult to imagine any situation in which a person could both rule and be ruled at one and the same time.

The unique nature of democratic polities, which might at first glance be taken as the strongest possible counter example, actually underscores this proposition. Consider, for example, a duly registered citizen at a polling station on election day, filling out a ballot. Few would deny that this person is acting as part of the sovereign tribunal, performing one of the classic functions (or subfunctions) of democratic governance. But, as all citizens of such polities know in their bones, the situation is somewhat ambiguous. While the real question we are asked to vote on may be whether or not the

community needs a new school, we may find it difficult to dissoci-
ate this question from our interests as subjects—as the ones who
will have to pay for the new school through a rise in our taxes, even
if we have no children. It may happen that, when it comes to
marking the secret ballot, one chooses to vote against the new
school because—well, because we may or may not need it, but
increased taxes are a burden that may finally make better education
for the community irrelevant, whether we have children or not ...
And so on.

A question asked of a citizen, in other words, is answered with
the heart of a subject. A sad situation it may be, if perhaps not
necessarily atypical. Just another mediocre democratic tragedy. But
what of the functions being performed? One ballot is cast, a single
document created, and to all eyes that ballot was cast in the performance of the governing function. Accordingly, it will rightly be
placed among the other ballots as part of a series within the fonds
of the appropriate agent of the sovereign. In a self-righteous mood,
one may carelessly throw the first stone, denouncing the ballot as
"merely private"—and so, by the criterion of *intention,* it may be.
But that is simply the way of democratic politics. We always wear
two hats and may or may not live up to our duties when performing
the ruling function. Still, the duality of functions *within* all citizens
does not in the least mean that they can perform both at the same
time. If one is voting, one is voting, whatever the intention that
underlies the result. The ambiguity is not in the function, but in our
nature as both citizens and subjects.

Consider, alternatively, the case of a public official issuing a
check to himself as a private subject of the sovereign. An official of
the department of social welfare, he signs the family allowance
checks that the department issues each month, and one of them
bears his own address. Not an ideal situation, perhaps, but not
uncommon. Though he wears two hats, he is performing a single
function at any given time—one as a public official, when he issues
the check, and one as a private subject, when he cashes it. Public
official and private subject may exist within a single person, but
only one of them can be creating or receiving and preserving any
given document at any given time, for document-generating functions can only be performed one at a time, and the functions of
ruling and being ruled are mutually exclusive.

Although it is thus impossible to generate public and private records concurrently, it is more than possible to generate them consecutively in the performance of different functions. Of course, as most working archivists know, it is often pointless to try to separate the two for purposes of archival description, since they are often found meshed together within a single filing scheme. However, the two *can* be distinguished theoretically, and perhaps even practically—at least by those archivists who enjoy the luxury of determining how the public and private records of public officials should be classified, filed, and scheduled for later disposition.

Consider, for example, the following situation. An archivist in a medium-sized city archives maintains a variety of documents in a cabinet next to her desk. For whatever reason, they are not classified as part of the archives' central filing system. The documents may be divided into three broad groups: those resulting from her work for the city; those resulting from her membership in and work for her regional professional association; and correspondence from colleagues. The job-related documents, moreover, can be divided into two sorts of files—those deriving from various projects she has been working on for the archives and those deriving from her service on a committee of the city clerk, to whom the city archives reports. Similarly, the association-related documents can be divided into those deriving from her work on the education committee and those deriving from her initial application and continuing individual membership.

Which, if any, of these documents are public records? A case can be made for considering them all public. The archivist is a legitimate officer of the city, itself a legitimate agent of the sovereign, and the documents were all made or received while working for the city. As well, the documents are preserved in an agency of the city, in equipment provided and owned by the city. Further, the documents all exist together within a single filing scheme.

The case, however, is not a strong one. First of all, as mentioned, the manner in which documents are filed may pose practical problems for archival description, but that has no bearing on their public or private nature. Even documents classified for placement in the official files can be *mis*classified, and scheduled documents *mis*scheduled. One can only know which is which by employing criteria external to the means of classification, filing, and scheduling. Moreover, if the documents are preserved in an agency of the city, that does indicate their custodial provenance. But custodial provenance is not at all the same as archival provenance, the primary concept for distinguishing public from private in archival terms. To urge that the documents are housed in equipment owned by the city may reinforce the city's custodial role, but it says as little about their public or private nature as the status of the archivist's dwelling—whether rented, borrowed, or owned—says about her nature as a citizen or subject or both.

Furthermore, while it is reasonable to characterize the archivist as an official of an agency of the sovereign, there is an ambiguity in saying that the documents were made or received while working for the city. The ambiguity lies in the word *while*, which can refer to the temporal period when a person is either (a) physically at the workplace or (b) engaging in the work that he or she is directly paid to do. The argument for considering as public records all documents made or received while working for the city equates these two meanings. In some instances this equation may be justifiable, but in many cases it is not. There are two angles from which this suggestion can be seen to be true. On the one hand, many agencies (these days, at least) are sensitive enough to realize that allowing at least a modicum of personal business to be conducted on agency time contributes to the well-being and overall job performance of its officials — whether that means allowing the secretary to accept emergency calls from home, the professional to accept calls from friends, or the head of state to accept calls from golfing buddies. On the other hand, any of these persons may take their work with them in the evening, performing in their own homes the work that they are directly paid to do—perhaps even to the extent of maintaining the resulting documents in their personal filing systems. Because this distinction between physical presence at the workplace and the performance of official functions is workable in any number of instances, those who would draw the meanings together bear the burden of demonstrating their case in any particular instance where the distinction seems to them inappropriate.

Considering the analysis offered in the present study, the fundamental question in the present case is this: given that the archivist makes or receives these various documents while physically at the workplace and that all of them are therefore records, in the performance of what particular functions are they generated, and do those functions derive from the sovereign authority or not? The archivist's project files are uncontroversially public, deriving from work that the city is mandated to do on behalf of the sovereign. So, too, the files deriving from the city clerk's committee, though with a twist. In this case, the archival provenance of the records is the city clerk's department, not the archives (assuming, again, that both may be considered as agencies in themselves). The reason for this is that the archivist, though an employee of the archives, was performing a function of the city clerk's department—an unofficial, though perhaps fairly common, form of secondment within the larger context of the city administration. It may well be that the city clerk is uninterested in this committee member's files and therefore makes no effort to have them placed in her department's file system. The resulting effect, however, is on their custodial, not on their archival, provenance.

However, in the performance of what function or functions were the archivist's correspondence and association files generated? Without much doubt, the correspondence received from colleagues must be considered nonpublic or private. It need not be marked "Personal and Confidential" to be so considered, for it does not relate to the functions performed by the city or the archives. It consists, rather, of that variously newsy, consolatory, congratulatory, gossipy, and generally fraternal brew of thought and sentiment that colleagues habitually share with one another. Such correspondence clearly derives from the free association of individual colleagues engaged in a common endeavor. Public matters may be spoken of, as in any conversation. But the very candor of such shared musings practically ensures that no public functions are being performed—at least not directly. If one colleague is indirectly examining another for a potential job through such correspondence, it may be considered manipulatory but is nonetheless "off the record." Accordingly, a function of one sort *disguised* as another must be taken at face value. With regard to archival provenance, the role presented is the role performed. An actual job offer, for example, would most likely require at some point an appropriate form of documentation signed over the colleague's official title.

Like her correspondence, the archivist's association files must also be considered private. The association is not an agent of the sovereign, because its constitution and bylaws will almost certainly have been registered with an agency of the sovereign under the terms of a Societies Act. Such registration, in our own system, typically confers the rights and duties whereby an organization is recognized by the sovereign as a legally valid subject. In some cases, of course, the governing body of a profession does have the status of a public agency, generally through its establishment by statute, because it performs a regulatory function on behalf of the sovereign. However, the present example assumes a situation more common among archival associations today.[64]

Still, if the professional association may thus be considered a private organization, there is a difference between the archivist's education committee and personal membership files. The situation parallels that of the archivist's public records, where one set of files was generated while performing a function of the archives and the other while performing a function of the city clerk's department. In this case, as well, two distinguishable functions are being performed. The education committee is a creature of the professional body. Having been instructed to perform a function or subfunction of that body, it serves as one of its agencies. With regard to the parent body, it parallels the relation of the archives or the city clerk's department to the city. Hence all those who serve on the education committee act as officials of the association, and the records they generate in the conduct of their function must therefore have the archival provenance of the association. It matters little whether the association cares to *claim* any such records for its own. After all, it may only be interested in receiving the final version of a set of educational guidelines ready for publication and may tacitly leave any decisions about the final disposition of working documents to the committee members who maintain them *custodially* on behalf of the association. Still, the archival provenance of such records clearly rests with the association on whose behalf they were made or received.

In contrast to the archivist's committee records, however, those of her membership must be considered part of her personal fonds. As a member of the association, pure and simple, she performs no functions or subfunctions on behalf of the association. The acts of joining, paying annual dues, receiving newsletters, and so forth are those of an individual member of the organization. Checks and letters received from her by the association form part of the organization's fonds, whereas receipts and letters received by her from the association form part of her personal fonds, just like the pay stubs on her monthly checks from the city, maintained as evidence of receipt in her own files.

A question naturally arises from this situation. Assume that the city had a policy of supplementing its holdings of documents made or received by its agents during the exercise of their functions through the acquisition of private records. What would be the status of the archivist's correspondence and membership files if, at the end of a long career, they were donated to the archives? Would they then be public or private?[65] It follows from the discussion so far that they would be *both*. They would be public as to custodianship (and most likely ownership as well, except perhaps for copyright), because they reside in a public agency. But their archival provenance would remain private. The question of possession is important, but it in no way affects the nature of the "person" who made or received the documents in the course of his, her, or its legitimate functions.

Consider another typical situation. An official of a central government body, such as the Privy Council in Canada, chairs an internal committee on a pressing constitutional accord. The committee is charged with studying the potential consequences of the accord and presenting relevant conclusions and recommendations. The official knows that the records resulting from the committee's deliberations will not be scheduled for continued retention, so they can be destroyed when they have served their immediate usefulness. However, considering them of importance to the national debate over the accord that has meanwhile been taking place, the official makes copies of the records and offers them to the National Archives as a donation of *private* records. The official insists that the records are private because he created them on his own as a concerned private person. Are they indeed private records?

First of all, it follows from the principles of archival provenance and agency that the records generated by the committee are public, because they were made or received by agents of the sovereign in the conduct of their legitimate function or subfunction. But what of the copies made by the chair of the committee and offered to the archives? It follows from the earlier discussion of provenance that these documents are private by *transmission*, since the chair offered them to the archives in his private capacity; he was not authorized to do so on behalf of the committee. However, because they were not authorized, it follows that the copies are inauthentic records.

Archivally, they are provenancially inauthentic. The official was able to make copies of them only because he had access to them in his capacity as an agent of the sovereign. As a private person, they were entirely beyond his reach; they could never have been generated in the course of his legitimate personal functions. In making the copies for dissemination, the official was performing an *illegitimate* function or subfunction of the sovereign, since the records were not meant to be retained—let alone disseminated—after their immediate usefulness to other agents of the sovereign had been exhausted. Accordingly, the documents offered by the official to the archives may be considered inauthentic public records masquerading as private records.

But what if the official had offered those copies to a newspaper that used them to produce an article on the accord and, after some years, donated them to the archives as part of its own fonds? What would their status be then, assuming that the newspaper's fonds may be taken as a legitimately private body of records? One's first impulse might be to urge that, though it would likely be more difficult to arrive at in practical terms, the verdict would remain the same: archivally, the documents are provenancially irregular, inauthentic public records. While being private by custodianship and transmission, they would remain inauthentic by the criterion of archival provenance.

This answer, though reasonable, does not exhaust the possibilities. It assumes that the provenance of a document attaches permanently to the person who first made or received and preserved it, whereas a case could be made for arguing that the archival provenance of a document can change over time. Since, in the present example, part of a newspaper's business is to gather such sources for potential articles, the archival provenance of the material could reasonably be placed with the newspaper. It was, after all, received in the regular conduct of one of the newspaper's functions, perhaps becoming part of a case file (if that is how the newspaper filed such material), which was eventually used to produce the article. It may possibly have generated letters from readers that were subsequently added to the file, as well, let alone correspondence from federal lawyers—both of which could have generated further records. In any event, the copied documents would have become an integral part of the newspaper's records. Since the newspaper's fonds is private, the leaked documents forming part of would it take on the same status, whether those documents were originally authentic or inauthentic. The legal concept of replevin may assume that the *ownership* of any document originally made or received in the conduct of the sovereign's affairs remains the property of the sovereign. Archivally, however, at least in terms of the present study, its provenance can change. In the present instance, documents that would be judged archivally inauthentic from the circumstances of their creation by the official—at least in the form in which they were offered to the National Archives—can be considered an (originally spurious) element of an authentic body of private records when sent to and received by a newspaper and subsequently transferred to the archives.[66]

The foregoing situations are meant to illustrate several typical differences and relations between the genesis of public and private records. While far from exhaustive, they do employ most of the concepts discussed in this chapter and sample a range of alternative situations. Among the latter, consideration has been given to the following: how a variety of public and private records can be generated by a single person while performing divergent roles; how a single public person can generate inauthentic records derived from public records but masquerading as private records; how, over time, inauthentic records can potentially become part of a body of private records; and how public records can become part of a body of private records, taking on their provenance.[67]

These situations can be rounded out by a brief examination of the relations between two persons, one public and one private, making or receiving documents in the course of their legitimate functions while sharing a common database. Imagine, for example, the department of energy in a province dependent on the health of the oil industry. One of its functions or subfunctions might be to keep track of both published and "grey" literature relevant to the industry and to provide periodic lists for its own researchers.[68] A major oil company in the province, wholly owned by private persons, also tries to keep track of such material for its own purposes. Realizing that each has ready access to material that might not be quite so readily available to the other when they work alone, the two decide to jointly fund and contribute entries to a common database that both may extract information from for their own purposes at any given time. Since the material so gathered by either organization could lead to disagreement among archivists about whether it is genuinely archival or gathered merely as reference material, let it be explicitly assumed that both the department of energy and the oil company have directed their library or "intelligence gathering" sections to generate lists of material for internal circulation; that is, such lists are genuine operational records for both organizations.

What would be the status of the lists extracted by each? Though the totality of information in the database would be jointly *owned*, it follows from the previous discussion that the archival provenance of the lists extracted from it would necessarily diverge. Those extracted by the department of energy would be public; those by the oil company, private. The database itself consists of documents —recorded information—rather than records. Only as the lists are extracted in the course of their divergent functions by each organization do they become records. As records, they reflect the public or private nature of the "person" who made or received them in the conduct of his, her, or its legitimate functions. The database itself may be considered both public and private through ownership; the records extracted from it, either public or private by the criterion of archival provenance.

This last situation, like the ones previously examined, hardly exhausts all the various possibilities. Nor is it meant to. The cases looked at are intended only to illustrate the main concepts examined earlier in this chapter and to suggest that one's approach to such situations depends as much on the concept of records one holds as on one's view of the nature of the person or persons generating *public* records. It is also hoped that such illustrations have shown at least some of the utility of the overall argument presented in this study, which may be stated as follows: public records can best be understood as documents made or received and preserved in the conduct of governance by the sovereign or its agents.

SUMMARY AND CONCLUSION

The subject of public records, of central importance to archivists, is large and complex. As such, it invites many questions from many angles. Because it is unlikely that such a subject can be encompassed empirically, a study of such records intended to be of use to archivists may reasonably apply the method of archival theory, for the results of such a broad study can be applied to a wide range of concerns and provide a basis for a variety of detailed explorations.

Because North American archivists do not share a common view of archival theory, however, and because such a method may seem unorthodox, it was necessary to outline the view of archival theory underlying this study. Accordingly, after examining common language and archival usage of the term, it was suggested that the notion of archival theory as conceptual knowledge resulting from the analysis of ideas can provide a distinct and comprehensive account of archival studies while illuminating questions regarding the relation between theory and practice, theoretical and empirical knowledge, and the descriptive and normative perspectives within archival theory.

This view of archival theory having been set forth, the discussion of records began by briefly examining etymology and historical usage. After this, the common archival meanings of *records* were placed in a hierarchy of terms comprising intelligence, information, documents, and records. The notion of records as documents made or received in the conduct of affairs was then coordinated with the traditional definition of archives, which is largely similar. This concept was also contrasted with Schellenberg's definition of archives as records judged worthy of permanent preservation for reference or research and deposited in an archival institution. After a lengthy discussion, it was determined that the traditional definition of archives offers all that Schellenberg's does and more. It was concluded, as a result, that records are best considered as archives in the traditional understanding.

The study then went on to examine the nature of public records. After reexamining the logical hierarchy of archival terms set out earlier, it was determined that public records are best considered as a subspecies or type of records based on the concept of person. This concept, it was demonstrated, provides a logical bridge between the concepts of records and public records. More specifically, it was shown that the provenance-based notion of person inhering in the definition of records offers the only reasonable criterion for moving from records to public records through division of the concept of records into its subcategories.

Given this framework, a substantive definition of public records was then offered. After examining common language and standard archival definitions, it was claimed that "the public" as a records creating person can best be defined as the sovereign, in contrast to private persons and organizations considered as the sovereign's subjects. This claim was then subjected to the critics, from whose arguments it emerged unscathed, and contrasted with Jenkinson's classification of public records, which was found wanting.

The equation of the public with the sovereign was then expanded on, refined, and tested within an archival context. Consideration was first given to the notion of provenance, the archival version of which was contrasted with the concepts of provenance as custodianship, transmission, and creation. The archival notion of provenance was then shown to include the concepts of function, legitimacy, and agency. As a result, it was concluded that public records can be defined as documents made or received in the conduct of its function or functions by the sovereign or its agents. This definition was then deepened by showing that the function of the sovereign is governance, and that this is so at all times and places. The theoretical and practical utility of this formulation was then explored by examining a number of representative situations. Given all that had gone before, it was finally concluded that public records are best considered as documents made or received and preserved in the conduct of governance by the sovereign or its agents.

NOTES

1. *Black's*, pp. 1135, 1227; *Funk & Wagnalls*, pp. 999, 1089. *People* derives from the Latin "populus," meaning the whole of the citizens, of which "public" is generally considered a possible but uncertain derivative. See Partridge, *Origins*, p. 483.

2. The qualifier "virtually" is used here to both acknowledge and ignore all those inhabitants who are subject to the laws but not party to their enactment — minors, resident aliens, visitors, and so forth. This is done not to slight them or to suggest that their number is small, but simply because they are largely irrelevant to the immediate discussion.

3. Though most readers of this study likely share a common political vocabulary, it seems only fair to state that my own understanding of the basic ideas of citizen, subject, state, and sovereignty employed here derive most directly from Thomas Hobbes, *Leviathan: Parts I and II*, ed. Herbert W. Schneider (Indianapolis, IN: Bobbs-Merrill, Library of Liberal Arts, 1958), and Jean Jacques Rousseau, *The Social Contract*, ed. Charles Frankel

(New York: Hafner Press, 1947). The works of Alexander Meiklejohn and Joseph Tussman have also been drawn on heavily, especially Meiklejohn's *Education Between Two Worlds* (New York: Atherton Press, Atheling, 1966) and Tussman's *Obligation and the Body Politic.*

Readers may want to balance these works by sampling some of the critics. Relatively brief treatments of particular concepts will be found in Daniel T. Rodgers, *Contested Truths: Keywords in American Politics Since Independence* (New York: Basic Books, 1987) and Albert Jay Nock, "Imposter Terms," in his *Free Speech and Plain Language,* pp. 285-304 (Freeport, NY: Books for Libraries Press, 1968). A more systematic treatment will be found in Robert Paul Wolff, *In Defense of Anarchism* (New York: Harper & Row, Harper Colophon Books, 1976).

4. A recent failure to make this distinction between citizens and subjects—not an isolated instance, and pointed out only because it lies most conveniently at hand—will be found in Anne Morddel, "The Delusion of Accountability," *Records Management Quarterly* 24 (July 1990): 42. Here "the public tax payer"—clearly, a reference to those *subject* to the law, since even nonvoting residents, visitors, and minors may well pay taxes—is confusedly equated with "the true 'employer' of all...ministers [of the Crown] and civil servants alike"—which can only refer to the sovereign citizens, in whose name Ministers of the Crown and civil servants perform their duties.

5. Bellardo and Bellardo, *A Glossary for Archivists,* p. 28; Evans, Harrison, and Thompson, "A Basic Glossary," p. 428. Another common definition, secondary to this one, is "records open to public inspection by law or custom" (ibid.). This "access" definition descends from the English common law definition mentioned earlier. Expressing a form of the action criterion centering on the concept of publicity, it is rightly considered secondary to the "person" definition, which was shown in the previous chapter to offer the best criterion for dividing records into public records and related categories. All the same, since the concept of access merits consideration, its relation to the present study is discussed in the Appendix.

6. Peterson and Peterson, *Law,* p. 12; Michael Cook, *The Management of Information from Archives* (Aldershot, England: Gower Publishing Company, 1986), p. 13. Both of the above also show that the constraints of tradition and legislation in the authors' respective countries have made for accumulations of records in their national repositories rather less, though in different ways, than the theoretical ideal of full and equal retention of records from all three organs. Generally speaking, it would seem, the lion's share of government records handled by archival agencies accrues from the executive or administrative branch. For the Canadian equivalent of these British and American examples, one may compare (perhaps with some injustice, considering the different dates) the *National Archives of*

Canada Act (Revised Statutes of Canada 1985, 3rd Supp. [1987, Ch. 1]) with the comparative extent of that archives' holdings of parliamentary, executive, and judicial records outlined in Terry Cook and Glen T. Wright, *General Guide Series 1983: Federal Archives Division* (Ottawa: Public Archives of Canada, 1983). To speak of the tripartite division of government as "traditional" is of course to draw on writers such as Aristotle and Montesquieu. See, for instance, J. A. Corry and J. E. Hodgetts, *Democratic Government and Politics*, 3rd ed., revised (Toronto: University of Toronto Press, 1959), pp. 90-92, where the basic distinctions are between the organ that makes the laws, the one that puts them into effect, and the one that determines in specific instances whether they have been upheld.

7. Bellardo and Bellardo, *Glossary*, p. 27; Evans, Harrison, and Thompson, "Glossary," p. 427. In a technical sense, "nonblack" would be the proper antithesis of "black," and "nonpublic" the proper antithesis of "public." Still, it is often useful—indeed, hardly avoidable—to bring such antitheses to life by giving them a recognizable name. It will prove useful in the discussion that follows to recall that the shades of grey of which life is said to be constituted do not in the least negate the distinction between white and black—contraries which, in fact, provide the basic distinction without which such shades could not even be conceived, let alone recognized. Sophisticated blurring of boundaries is often necessary, but remains at all times dependent on fundamental distinctions; sophistication rides the shoulders of simplicity.

All the same, though "private" may not have any positive meaning etymologically, it is acceptable because today it is a substantive term in its own right—not simply the antithesis of "public," as nonblack is the antithesis of black (as hinted at the distinction between citizens and subjects). For the etymologically correct derivation of "private," see Luciana Duranti, "Diplomatics: New Uses for an Old Science (Part III)," *Archivaria* 30 (Summer 1990): 14. An account of the complex history of the term in English usage over the past several centuries, and incidentally of its undeniably substantive character, will be found in Williams, *Keywords*, pp. 203-204. See also Heather MacNeil, *Without Consent: The Ethics of Disclosing Personal Information in Public Archives* (Metuchen, NJ: Society of American Archivists and Scarecrow Press, 1992), pp. 1-2.

8. Rousseau, *The Social Contract*, pp. 50-55. See also Alexander Meiklejohn, "The First Amendment Is An Absolute," in his *Alexander Meiklejohn, Teacher of Freedom: A Collection of His Writings and A Biographical Study*, ed. Cynthia Stokes Brown (Berkeley, CA: Meiklejohn Civil Liberties Institute, Studies in Law and Social Change No. 2, 1981), p. 247. It is worth noting in this context that "government" is etymologically derived from Latin and Greek terms meaning "to steer or pilot" (Partridge, *Origins*, p. 262). This meaning derives from the ancient metaphor of the ship of state and is so recognized by modern jurists, who rightly note that the government must

accordingly be considered "but an agency of the state," as the helmsman is but an agent of the captain or owner of a ship (*Black's*, p. 695).

9. Evans, Harrison, and Thompson, "Glossary," p. 427.

10. There may be some useful technical reason for distinguishing organizations from institutions, but whatever difference there may be between the two is irrelevant to the argument being developed here. Accordingly, *organizations* is used as a generic term for all groups of subjects who have bound themselves together to form what Hobbes would call an "artificial person"—or, more precisely, in his fine-meshed logic net, "regular, dependent political systems," meaning artificial persons subject to the sovereign and gaining their existence therefrom by letters patent or some other lawful means, such as business corporations (*Leviathan*, pp. 180-92). Such organizations fall within the broader category of juridical, as distinguished from physical, persons (see Duranti, "Diplomatics," *Archivaria* 28: 25, note 20).

11. Evans, Harrison, and Thompson, "Glossary," pp. 426, 427; "manuscripts" are often considered the equivalent of "papers" so defined (ibid.). Bellardo and Bellardo define private records as those of nongovernmental provenance, which include (from their definition of records) documents made or received by organizations *and* individuals (*Glossary*, pp. 27, 28). In itself, this move would seem to eliminate the dichotomy between private records and papers found in Evans, Harrison, and Thompson. However, they complicate matters both by defining private or personal papers as those of individuals and by defining papers as documents of personal or family provenance—the latter being contrasted with those generated by organizations, which in this instance they call records, and thereby eliminate from the definition of records the documents of individuals that they elsewhere include (ibid., p. 25). Clearly, room exists here for further work toward consistency.

12. Robert L. Brubaker, "Archival Principles and the Curator of Manuscripts," *American Archivist* 29 (October 1966): 507.

13. For an overview of these developments, see Eastwood, "Unity and Diversity in the Development of Archival Science in North America," pp. 4-6. A longer tale is told in Berner's *Archival Theory and Practice in the United States.* As well, a glance at the classical definitions of archives provided earlier shows that only the Dutch exclude documents generated by private persons (and, it would appear, nongovernmental organizations as well), while Brenneke too includes both physical and juridical persons in his definition of archives (see Schellenberg, *Modern Archives*, pp. 12-13)—all of which underscores the historically accidental nature of the North American split between records and papers. One strong indication that this conceptually needless split has been all but healed will be found in the recent legal codification in both the United States and Canada of the term "personal *records.*" On the American *Presidential Records Act* (1980), see

Maygene F. Daniels, "Introduction to Archival Terminology," in *A Modern Archives Reader,* ed. Daniels and Walch, p. 337, note 5; see also the *National Archives of Canada Act* (1987), Secs. 2, 4 (1).

14. Terry Eastwood, "The Disposition of Ministerial Papers," *Archivaria* 4 (Summer 1977): 14.

15. Helen Samuels, "Who Controls the Past," *American Archivist* 49 (Spring 1986): 110-11.

16. In *Archival Documents: Providing Accountability Through Recordkeeping,* edited by Sue McKemmish and Frank Upward (Melbourne: Ancora Press, 1993), pp. 36, 37. See also note 7 above.

17. This conclusion is almost arrived at in Cook and Procter's discussion of the nature of archives and the consequences for description (*A Manual of Archival Description,* pp. 3-5). Noting the difference between organic accumulations of records that generally end up in the archives of a sponsoring agency responsible for them and single items that often end up in so-called manuscript repositories, the authors come close to concluding that the only real difference between the two kinds of material—at least for the sake of description—is that while the former may be described collectively, the latter can only be described individually. In other words, the difference between the two lies more in the level at which they can be described than in any supposed difference in their fundamental nature.

18. The standard classification of archives in the United Kingdom, Jenkinson's scheme is now most readily available in three sources: *A Manual of Archive Administration,* pp. 191-97; "General Report of a Committee on the Classification of English Archives" [1936], in his *Selected Writings,* pp. 122-46; and "The Classification and Survey of English Archives" [1943], in his *Selected Writings,* pp. 196-207.

19. Jenkinson, "General Report of a Committee on the Classification of English Archives," p. 125.

20. Jenkinson, *Manual,* p. 196. While Jenkinson speaks here of serving a public "function," this term does not affect his meaning when speaking of "interests"; functions may be thought of as areas of activity, so that a "public" function would be one that furthers the public interest.

21. These comments about an apparent pragmatic bent in some of Jenkinson's theoretical offerings doubtless "tread on the quicksand of perception," as Terry Eastwood nicely puts it in "Going Nowhere in Particular: The Association of Canadian Archivists Ten Years After," *Archivaria* 21 (Winter 1985-86): 187. Though not directly relevant to the present discussion, such comments are based on long contemplation of this portion of Jenkinson's work and are offered as no more than a possible explanation of his line of reasoning. For a searching discussion of pragmatic compromise, see Tussman, *Obligation and the Body Politic,* pp. 114-18.

22. The discussion here relates to the intent or purpose of the organization, which should be distinguished from the motives of the organization's

members. Although the two might be expected to coincide, they need not, and any lack of such correspondence does not affect the point made here about organizational purposes. There may be officers of civil liberties organizations, for example, who volunteer their time and talents with the intent of gaining some personal "advantage or satisfaction," such as fame, fortune, and the love of beautiful women (as Freud would put it), though one suspects that they are often disappointed. Nevertheless, personal successes and disappointments of this sort hardly affect the purposes of the organization, which is not the sum of its individual members and officers but a body unto itself with its own purposes, as set down in its constitution.

23. John Dixon, former president of the British Columbia Civil Liberties Association, letter to the author, August 20, 1989. Dixon's formulation draws on Joseph Tussman, *The Burden of Office: Agamemnon and Other Losers* (Vancouver: Talonbooks, 1989), pp. 15-25. Civil liberties organizations are mentioned here partly because they are the type of voluntary organization with which I am most familiar and partly because they seem to provide an incisive example of the relations between public and private interests and effects. If the example seems somehow strained or inappropriate, readers may prefer to reflect on their own experience with voluntary organizations of whatever sort.

24. When considering public intentions and effects of this sort, it should be noted that altruistic acts in general, though usually contributing nothing to the actor's private "advantage or satisfaction," are not for that reason to be considered *public* in effect, as this notion has been characterized above. It has been assumed so far, following Jenkinson, that private intents and effects are self-interested or self-aggrandizing. However, if public effects are defined as those affecting the *whole* of the sovereign's subjects (or the members of the sovereign tribunal itself, as when suggesting that civil liberties organizations promote freedom of speech for the *citizens* of a state), then it follows that private effects—and, by implication, private intents— must be defined as those affecting only a *part* of the whole of the sovereign's *subjects,* whether or not the intent of the actor or the effect of the act is "selfish." In other words, an altruistic act can be either public or private in effect, depending on whether it affects either the whole of the sovereign's subjects or a part of those subjects, whether an individual or a group.

25. Jenkinson, "General Report," pp. 126, 132-33. This apparently felt necessity to reconcile historical changes in the creators of certain series of records with what he considered a necessarily static theoretical classifica- tion of records creators that would do justice to the records of the present day may well point toward Jenkinson's decision to accept what has here been characterized as a pragmatic compromise. Unfortunately, at times he comes perilously close to conflating the historical with the theoretical, which could result in no end of confusion, as when he contrasts the private

interests that at some time in the past brought an organization into existence with the public interests that they are, at present, considered to further
(ibid., p. 133).

26. This intuitive sense, one might suppose, has much to do with our
juridical environment, as exemplified by the formal division of positive
domestic law into the spheres of public and private based on the interests
involved. See, for example, Gerald Gall, *The Canadian Legal System*, 2nd ed.
(Toronto: Carswell Legal Publications, Carswell Student Edition, 1983), pp.
19-20. For a definition of "juridical," which is broader than but includes
the law, see Duranti, "Diplomatics: New Uses for an Old Science (Part II),"
Archivaria 29 (Winter 1989-90): 5.

27. See Chapter 4.

28. Duranti, "Diplomatics (Part III)," p. 16.

29. Ibid., emphasis added. To be fair, it should be noted that the author
qualifies this statement by adding that "in so doing, [that public person is]
vested with the exercise of some sovereign power." This statement seems
to point in the same direction as the present discussion, so that there may
not be any real disagreement, finally, between diplomatic and archival
theory on the nature of public persons. However, this qualification is given
only as a hint in passing. No suggestion is given about what this clause
may refer to in substance, the rest of the discussion stressing rather the
relativity of the concept of public person from one juridical system to
another (ibid., pp. 14-18).

30. The indication that diplomatists believe both that "public" should
be defined relative to any given system and that "there is no clear distinction between public and private law in any juridical system" suggests a
certain ambivalence at the root of the diplomatic treatment of public and
private persons (ibid., p. 16). This ambivalence is further suggested by
diplomatists' apparent belief that the substantive notion of the concept of
person is subject to "philosophic conceptions which may differ within the
same juridical system" (which seems true enough), while assuming that
the forms and procedures enacted by public persons can somehow be
discerned as public without a prior substantive definition of "public"
(ibid., p. 17).

31. See Chapter 4.

32. Ibid., note 9.

33. *Funk & Wagnalls*, p. 1085.

34. This is the sense in which Jenkinson, perhaps unfortunately, seems
to have understood the term *provenance*—summarily dismissing its applicability to the principle that bodies of documents created or received by
distinct entities should be maintained separately (see his *Manual*, pp.
97-98). Michael Cook comments on Jenkinson's usage in *Archives Administration: A Manual for Intermediate and Smaller Organizations and for Local
Government* (Folkestone, England: Dawson, 1977), p. 223, note 9.

35. Diplomatic provenance is thus akin to what was earlier called "legal provenance," in that both focus on the entity from which documents are issued (see Chapter 4, note 10). For a precise and illuminating account of what diplomatists mean by "authorship," see Duranti, "Diplomatics (Part III)."

36. As hinted here, archivists generally deal with series of records rather than individual items. However, a single (and admittedly mundane) record is here used by way of example for the sake of simplicity—and therefore, one may hope, clarity.

37. See Debra Barr, "Protecting Provenance: Response to the Report of the Working Group on Description at the Fonds Level," *Archivaria* 28 (Summer 1989): 141-42.

38. The notion of a sphere or area of activity, as used here, may be contrasted with the notion of action discussed in the previous chapter. In that earlier discussion, the focus was on the specific actions of making, receiving, and preserving documents. Here the focus is on the larger spheres of activity in which those specific actions take place and toward which they contribute.

39. For recent discussions of function, activity, and related concepts, see Duranti, "Diplomatics (Part III)," p. 19, note 10; and Frances Fournier, "Faculty Papers: Appraisal For Acquisition and Selection," (Master of Archival Studies thesis, University of British Columbia, 1990), p. 17 and note 15, pp. 35-36. Bellardo and Bellardo define function as "an activity directed at carrying out a mission for an organization" (*A Glossary for Archivists*, p. 16).

40. See, for example, Canadian Council of Archives, *The Canadian Archival System: A Report on the National Needs and Priorities of Archives* (Ottawa: Canadian Council of Archives, May 1989). The flexibility of the concept of function noted in the present study may be compared to the "maximalist" and "minimalist" views of the concept of fonds noted in Duchein, "The Principle of Provenance in Archives Administration," pp. 90-94.

41. For the diplomatic definition of competence, see Duranti, "Diplomatics [Part III]," p. 19, note 10. The use of the terms *competence* and *legitimacy* in the present context should be distinguished from their use in Max Weber's influential work. On the one hand, his discussion of legitimacy bears close resemblance to the concept of legitimacy or competence employed here. On the other hand, however, his notion of competence is far narrower than the diplomatic concept, being closely bound to the legal structure of bureaucracy, particularly in the modern world. See Max Weber, *The Theory of Social and Economic Organization*, trans. A. M. Henderson and Talcott Parsons, ed. Talcott Parsons (New York: The Free Press, 1964), pp. 330-31, 343-44, 360.

42. Duranti, "Diplomatics," *Archivaria* 28: 17.

43. Considering the complexities involved in arriving at a satisfactory definition of records, the term *nonrecords* should perhaps be used only, if at all, with great care. It would seem, at any rate, that substantive description of the various qualities that records may have enriches terminology far more than negation, which can nonetheless be a useful shorthand for indicating where analysis has ended for the time being. The use of "nonrecords" when referring to transitory records is discussed above in Chapter 3, note 64.

44. Duranti, "Diplomatics," *Archivaria* 28: 17-18.

45. The distinction between authenticity and genuineness thus eliminates a potential ambiguity in the concept of legitimacy, which can refer to both competence and propriety. Strictly speaking, therefore, *legitimate* in the sense of competent should qualify "affairs" rather than "conduct" in the phrase, "the conduct of affairs."

46. See p. 117 above.

47. *Black's*, p. 62. See also Tussman, *Obligation and the Body Politic*, pp. 58-76.

48. Needless to say, this list of organizational forms is hardly exhaustive. The enormous task of listing them all, let alone determining a satisfactory classification, may be imagined by noting that one recent study puts the number of governmental units at the local level in the United States at some 81,000—comprising an unidentified number of forms. See H. G. Jones, *Local Government Records: An Introduction to Their Management, Preservation, and Use* (Nashville, TN: American Association for State and Local History, 1980), pp. x, 107.

49. That we call many of these agencies *quasi*-governmental bodies (usually in the phrases "quasi-judicial bodies" and "quasi-administrative bodies") doubtless reflects to some extent our sense of their relative distance from the sovereign in terms of legislated authority. But it may also reflect a measure of confusion about the difference between what is called "the government" and the sovereign—or, to put it more exactly, the difference between those agencies that derive their powers directly from the constitution and the source of the constitution itself. If we are unsure of the exact relationship between the government and the sovereign, while sensing that many boards and commissions do not have equal status with the government, it may be that we tend to relegate such bodies to the conceptually fuzzy land of "quasi-ness."

50. See, for instance, Max J. Evans, "Authority Control: An Alternative to the Record Group Concept," *American Archivist* 49 (Summer 1986): 249-61.

51. *Black's*, pp. 62-64, 326. It will have been noted that the relation between the sovereign and organizations such as universities, hospitals, and corporations inevitably changes across societies and over time. In the

present context, the concern is with contemporary English-speaking democracies alone.

52. With regard to the principle of agency, the argument once put forth by a number of archivists that the *constitutional* nature of the office of President of the United States makes each incumbent's records purely private is not entirely persuasive (see J. Frank Cook, "'Private Papers' of Public Officials," *American Archivist* 38 [July 1975]: 301). After all, as pointed out above, a distinction must be made between (a) those agencies or offices that derive their authority directly from the constitution and (b) the source of the constitution itself — namely, the sovereign citizens. With the passing of the *Presidential Records Act* in the United States and the *National Archives Act* in Canada, some archivists may have concluded that this issue is now dead, since both acts point toward the public nature of the records of high-ranking officials. However, it is useful to recall that the winning of battles does not ensure the winning of wars and the winning of wars does not ensure the triumph of principles. For an update on the legislation mentioned above, see Peterson and Peterson, *Law*, pp. 15-16; National Archives and Records Administration, *Personal Papers of Executive Branch Officials: A Management Guide* (Washington, DC: National Archives and Records Administration, Management Guide Series, 1992); and Charles Mackinnon and Robert Czerny, "Managing the Records of a Minister's Office," *The Archivist* 16 (September-October 1989): 2-4.

53. Since it has been determined that legitimacy or competence affects the status of provenance (authentic or inauthentic) but not its existence, "legitimate" will be excluded from here on as part of the definition.

54. Though not wanting to claim that my own understanding of democratic sovereignty is universally applicable in the present context, I do not for that reason suggest that some such argument could not be defended. Among other things, one need only contemplate for a moment the consequences of applying to all polities the idea of the social contract, not as a historical concept, but as an analytical tool for laying bare the logic of political society—which seems very much to have been what Hobbes and Rousseau were aiming toward, though often interpreted rather differently (see, for example, Morris R. Cohen, *The Meaning of Human History* [Lasalle, IL: Open Court, The Paul Carus Lectures Series 6, 1947], pp. 238-45). A successful development of this line of thought, however, would not substantially affect the argument offered here and is perhaps best left to the political philosophers in any case.

55. F. H. Hinsley, *Sovereignty* (London: C. A. Watts & Co., 1966), p. 5. I take this statement to be particularly authoritative because it comes from an expert who is at pains to *deny* that the undisputed existence of such political systems in all societies demonstrates the universality of a certain technical version of the modern concept of sovereignty. He concedes that such systems are universal in order to deny their relevance to the technical

notion of sovereignty with which he disagrees. The generic notion of sovereignty employed here is accordingly justified by its appeal to the simple fact of an ultimate source of authoritative or legitimate governance, with no technical complications implied. See also S. N. Eisenstadt, *The Political Systems of Empires* (New York: The Free Press of Glencoe, 1963), pp. 5-6, who maintains that this position represents a consensus among scholars across all relevant disciplines; and Posner, *Archives in the Ancient World*, pp. 3-4. Both of the latter authors also delineate what they consider the constant subfunctions into which the broad function of governance may be divided.

56. Diplomatists complement the notion of competence (discussed above) with that of responsibility, defined as the obligation to answer for an act (see Duranti, "Diplomatics [Part III]," p. 8). The concept of responsibility is not included in the present discussion because it does not apply to the sovereign as defined here. It applies only to the sovereign's agents. As the first and final authority in any given polity, the sovereign can never be held responsible, because the obligation to answer can only be borne by an entity that is in some way subordinate to another. Since the supreme authority is in no way subordinate, it is in no way responsible in this sense. If, for example, a constitutional monarch can be held responsible in some ways, it cannot for that very reason be considered the sovereign *in those particular ways.* To the extent that the Queen of England is responsible to Parliament, she is not in fact the *sovereign,* at least as the concept is defined here. Sovereignty, in this instance, would reside in the citizens of England, on whose behalf Parliament sits. In other words, while the present study may in some cases lead away from particular juridical entities such as queens and emperors toward a more conceptual view of the sovereign, it takes seriously the adage that "the king can do no wrong" (cf. Duranti, ibid., p. 9).

57. Wolff, *In Defense of Anarchism,* p. 4.

58. Logically, it would seem, there are two sources of recognition for the sovereign's authority within any given political system, one internal and the other external. The recognition may exist *within* a given polity, by the persons obligated to obey the sovereign, or it may come from the other sovereigns with which any given sovereign may form part of an international political system. In other words, one must look both to constitutional and international law or their equivalent (where they exist) for empirical answers to questions about the legitimacy of the sovereign in any given polity. It will have been noted that *legitimacy* in the present context refers essentially to a higher order of competence, as discussed earlier in relation to provenance—the legitimacy of a mandate, as it were, in contrast with the legitimacy of the functions by which a mandate is realized.

59. A further element could be added at this point; namely, the particular areas of activity governed by the sovereign's authority in any given

polity—what might be called the subfunctions of governance. As noted above, organizations such as schools will be considered public—that is, agents of the sovereign—wherever governance is taken to include authority over the development of the minds of its subjects. Similarly, religious organizations will be considered public wherever governance of the spirit is considered a subfunction of the sovereign. For a discussion of the sovereign "teaching power" in democracies, see Joseph Tussman, *Government and the Mind* (New York: Oxford University Press, 1977).

60. It seems only fair to suggest at this point how such theoretical considerations might possibly be applied to empirical questions. Consider, for instance, the claim made by historians of medieval England that the distinction between public and private did not exist before, say, the fourteenth century (see Pollock and Maitland, *The History of English Law Before the Time of Edward I*, vol. 2, pp. 230-31; and S. B. Chrimes, *An Introduction to the Administrative History of Medieval England*, 3rd ed. [Oxford: Blackwell, 1966], pp. 65, 156). Rather than reply with empirical claims, one could ask the following counterquestions by way of clarifying exactly what claim it is that they are making: Does the fact that the king's domains were *perceived* as merely private demonstrate that no distinction was in fact made between what "belonged" to the king and what "belonged" to his *subjects*? Did they recognize a distinction between ruler and ruled, either in principle or in practice? If so, does it matter substantially if they recognized such a distinction but did not use the terms in vogue today? On what grounds do we claim that what we call "private" is bound to the quality of "ownership" — for do we not, to use our own terms, distinguish between what is owned by the public and what is owned by private persons and groups? To ask such questions is not to suggest that the answers to them are self-evident. The questions suggest only that, while theory cannot in itself provide empirical evidence, it *can* provide ways to question and interpret existing empirical investigations and suggest further lines of inquiry.

61. Considering the earlier discussions about the nature of records and provenance, this definition is but an application for present purposes of the various elements that must be accounted for in any definition of a subspecies or type of records based on a particular kind of records creator.

62. This impossibility, as suggested above, exists only at the level of single actions; action by action, one either rules or is ruled. "To rule," in other words, is a different sort of verb than, say, "to kick," for one can both kick and be kicked at the same time.

63. See p. 129 above.

64. As an example of the rationale for including self-governing professional bodies under a freedom of information and protection of privacy act, see Barry Jones, "The Extension of Citizens' Information and Privacy Rights to all Public Bodies in British Columbia: Report Presented to the Honorable Colin Gabelmann, Attorney General and Chair, Cabinet Cau-

cus Committee on Information and Privacy" (Victoria, February 1, 1993), pp. 20-21.

65. This question is raised in Bernard Weilbrenner, "L'homme politique et ses archives: papiers publics ou privés?" *Archives* 10 (Décembre 1978): 35-36.

66. Although this conclusion does, I think, follow reasonably from the analysis of records and provenance set forth in the present study, it is offered here as more of a suggestion than anything. As implied in the above example, determining the public or private status of records depends to a large extent on one's views about the nature of records and provenance— not just on one's views about the nature of public and private records creators. Since the basic concepts used by archivists (to hazard the refrain once more) are open to a good deal more analysis than they have received so far, and the notions of records and provenance employed in the present study assume the traditional interpretation, dogmatism is hardly warranted in such cases. Still, the notion of changing provenance is familiar, if still conceptually debated, territory for archivists with regard to records produced by one public agency within a given jurisdiction and subsequently used in its affairs by a second or third agency. The newspaper scenario discussed above, it could be argued, simply applies a twist to this familiar situation.

67. To be exhaustive here would require, among other things, the description of situations where the opposite results may occur; that is, where the roles of public and private in each of the situations were reversed, so that (for example) it could be shown how *private* records can take on the provenance of *public* records in certain circumstances. Although confident that the present analysis could support such exhaustive exemplification, I have hesitated to do so for fear of needlessly bloating this study, while hoping that a set of representative situations will be enough to clarify the overall argument.

68. Grey literature has been defined by one commentator as material not available through normal bookselling channels. See David N. Wood, "Management of Grey Literature," in *Management of Recorded Information: Converging Disciplines; Proceedings of the International Council on Archives' Symposium on Current Records; National Archives of Canada, Ottawa, May 15-17 1989*, comp. Cynthia J. Durance (Munich: K. G. Saur, 1990), pp. 61-62.

Appendix

Access to Information

In chapter 5, the attempt to provide a substantive definition of "the public" led to equating it with the sovereign. Some effort was made to elaborate on and test that equation. However, the theoretical utility of any concept derives partly from its ability to frame related issues in new and effective ways. Toward this end, the reader is invited to consider the notion of access to information from the perspective of the public as sovereign.

Public records are commonly defined by archivists not only as government records but also as records open to the public. While the former notion is somewhat more common than the latter these days, it was not always so. In fact, until the middle of the nineteenth century in Great Britain, public records referred exclusively to those open to inspection by the public, considered as the aggregate of the sovereign's subjects. Such records were traditionally referred to as "the people's evidences"—the source on which all subjects might draw as evidence of rights requiring establishment or defense against either the Crown or other subjects.[1]

However, with the rising consciousness of a democratic polity in the wake of the American and French revolutions over the past hundred and fifty years, the notion of "the people's evidences" has slowly expanded. Records once considered open to the public as individual subjects of the sovereign are now, with access to (or "freedom of") information acts, also seen as open to the public as citizens holding membership in the sovereign tribunal. While still providing evidence about the rights of individuals, such records are now seen as providing citizens with evidence of the work performed on their behalf and in their name by their delegated agents. Public records, it might be said, are now seen as the arsenal of the polis—the material means by which free citizens gain much of the information necessary to "exercise judgment on behalf of a consciously self-governed community."[2]

Such, at any rate, is a reasonable interpretation of recent federal acts in the United States and Canada from the point of view adopted in this study—namely, the public as the sovereign. These acts—the U. S. *Freedom of Information Act* and the Canadian *Access to Information Act*—are instructive in both their similarities and differences.[3] The main similarities between the two acts reside in the basic principle on which they are founded and in the way that they qualify that principle. Both acts adopt the principle that all information generated by the executive branch of government should be open to the public from the moment of creation or receipt. Access to information is thus seen as a right, not a privilege, from which it follows that any withholding of such information must be clearly justified.

In setting out the categories of information that are exempt from immediate access, and thereby qualifying the principle of openness, the two acts are also similar. Both outline a number of exempt categories that fall within two broad areas where confidentiality is deemed necessary: sensitive areas of policy and procedure relating to the functioning of the government, such as national defense and law enforcement, and the personal lives and commercial affairs of individuals.[4] In these two areas of exemption from the principle of immediate access are found once again the distinction between the public as the sovereign—whose delegated agents require a sphere of confidentiality in order to carry out their responsibilities—and the public as the aggregate of the sovereign's subjects, individually and in corporate groups—who require a measure of privacy in order to carry on their lawful affairs without undue intrusion.

The distinction between these two senses of "the public" also surfaces in the stipulations laid down about *who* shall be granted such access. On this score, the two acts seem to differ. The American act is wide open, stating that virtually anyone and everyone should be granted free access to government information. The Canadian act, on the other hand, limits this right to citizens and permanent residents.[5] This difference is only apparent, for the two acts could not be founded on the same basic principle and differ on the category of persons to whom that principle is applied. Whatever the reason for the difference, it seems clear that the American act may perhaps be worded more generously than the Canadian, but that the Canadian act is more precise, relating the principle of free access to government information directly to the category of persons to whom such access applies—and thereby clarifying the basic principle. To put it succinctly, the Canadian provision that access to information applies only to citizens and permanent residents sends a clear message that such access is both warranted and desirable in order that the sovereign citizens may truly have the means to govern themselves. The extension of this right to noncitizen permanent residents reduces to some extent the "purity" of the argument that the principle of free access derives from the sovereign citizens' need for evidence and information. Still, there is a vast difference between permanent residents, who have made a commitment to the polis, and all other noncitizens. This commitment, which entails a personal stake in the well-being of the state, goes a long way toward justifying the extension of this right to permanent residents.

In other words, access to information is a right of citizens, not subjects. The members of the sovereign tribunal have an unchallenged right to information generated by their agents, because that information is generated in their name. To extend that right to subjects and foreigners, as in the American act, may be wise, insofar as the information brought to light by such persons can assist the sovereign citizens in their ruling work. But any such extension must be considered a tactical provision, not a fundamental element of the principle itself.[6]

The position adopted here might be contrasted with that taken by some members of the Canadian historical profession, who have called it "silly" and "irritating" that the provision of access should apply only to Canadian citizens and permanent residents. Ignoring the difference between immediate access to current information and access to "historical" information of the sort housed in archival repositories that has been and still is open to citizens, subjects, foreigners, and all other comers, they have viewed the new law as threatening to "reverse a long and honorable tradition in Canada of allowing access to our historical records to citizens of any country."[7] This may perhaps be so. However, from the perspective adopted in this study, it would be both clearer and more persuasive to argue that since such researchers have contributed over the years to the stock of information and ideas needed by the sovereign citizens in order to rule effectively, they should be allowed access in order that they may continue to do so.

NOTES

1. Great Britain, Public Record Office, *First Report of the Deputy Keeper of the Public Records* (London, 1840), p. 67. Comment on the changing usage of "public records" during the nineteenth century will be found in the Grigg Report, pp. 8-9 (for a full bibliographical citation, see Introduction, note 9). For the archival definition of "public" as records accessible to the public, see Chapter 5, note 5.

2. Graham Wallas, as quoted in Tussman, *Obligation and the Body Politic,* p. 10. While expressing his faith that truth will always win out in a fair fight, which one need not share, James Madison once expressed something close to this idea when he urged that: "A popular Government without popular information, or the means of acquiring it, is but a Prologue to a Farce or a Tragedy; or, perhaps both. Knowledge will forever govern ignorance: And a people who mean to be their own Governors must arm themselves with the power which Knowledge gives" (as quoted in Arthur Schleisinger, Jr., "Foreword," *The Records of Federal Officials: A Selection of Materials from the National Study Commission on Records and Documents of Federal Officials,* ed. Anna Kasten Nelson [New York: Garland Publishing, 1978], p. ix).

3. 5 *United States Code,* Sec. 552; *Revised Statutes of Canada* 1985, Ch. A-1.

4. See Peterson and Peterson, *Law,* pp. 45-60; and Robert J. Hayward, "Federal Access and Privacy Legislation and the Public Archives of Canada," *Archivaria* 18 (Summer 1984): 50.

5. "Permanent residents," that is, as defined in the *Immigration Act,* which limits this category to persons who (a) have been granted landing (defined as "lawful permission to come into Canada to establish permanent residence"), (b) have not become Canadian citizens, and (c) have not ceased to be permanent residents (*Revised Statutes of Canada* 1985, Ch. I-2, Sec. 2).

6. The argument that extending such access to all subjects and foreigners may help the sovereign citizens perform their ruling function also applies to American and Canadian constitutional provisions for freedom of speech. This particular right also derives from the citizens' need for ideas and information necessary for the successful performance of their job as rulers. Since evidence about the performance of their agents and information about policies are two results of access to "information" intended by the citizens in enacting access legislation, provision for the free interplay of ideas that may lead to new policy is the primary intent of the constitutional guarantee of "free speech" (see John Dixon, "Freedom of Speech as a Fundamental Right," position paper adopted by the Board of Directors

of the British Columbia Civil Liberties Association, March 13, 1989, especially pp. 9-22). It will be noted that the tactical extension of access to subjects and foreigners provides an even stronger reason for extending this right to permanent residents.

7. Robert Craig Brown, "Government and Historian: A Perspective on Bill C43," *Archivaria* 13 (Winter 1981-82): 122. On the general question of research access to *personal* information in archives, see MacNeil, *Without Consent*.

Selected Bibliography

American Assembly. "The Records of Public Officials." *American Archivist* 38 (July 1975): 329-36.

Andrews, Charles M. "Archives." In *Annual Report of theAmerican Historical Association for the Year 1913.* 2 vols. Vol. 1, pp. 262-65. Washington, DC: 1915.

Archer, John H. "The Public Records in Saskatchewan." *Journal of the Society of Archivists* 2 (April 1960): 16-25.

Aristotle. *Aristotle: Selections.* Edited by W. D. Ross. New York: Charles Scribner's Sons, 1927.

Association of Canadian Archivists. Education Committee. "Guidelines for the Development of a Two-Year Curriculum for a Master of Archival Studies Programme (December 1988)." *Archivaria* 29 (Winter 1989-90): 128-41.

Atherton, Jay. "From Life Cycle to Continuum: Some Thoughts on the Records Management-Archives Relationship." *Archivaria* 21 (Winter 1985-86): 43-51.

Auerbach, Isaac L. "Future Development in Data Processing." In *Information Science: Search for Identity,* pp. 215-20. Edited by Anthony Debons. New York: Marcel Dekker, 1974.

Austin, John. *Lectures on Jurisprudence or the Philosophy of Positive Law.* 5th ed. Revised and edited by Robert Campbell. London: John Murray, 1885.

Bain, George W. "State Archival Law: A Content Analysis." *American Archivist* 46 (Spring 1983): 158-74.

Baker, J. H. *An Introduction to English Legal History.* 2nd ed. London: Butterworths, 1979.

Barr, Debra. "Protecting Provenance: Response to the Report of the Working Group on Description at the Fonds Level." *Archivaria* 28 (Summer 1989): 141-45.

Barzun, Jacques, and Graff, Henry F. *The Modern Researcher.* 3rd ed. New York: Harcourt Brace Jovanovich, 1977.

Basu, Purnendu. *Archives and Records: What Are They?* New Delhi: National Archives of India, 1960.

Bearman, David, and Lytle, Richard. "The Power of the Principle of Provenance." *Archivaria* 21 (Winter 1985-86): 14-27.

Bellardo, Lewis J., and Bellardo, Lynn Lady, comps. *A Glossary for Archivists, Manuscript Curators, and Records Managers.* Chicago: Society of American Archivists, Archival Fundamentals Series, 1992.

Berner, Richard. *Archival Theory and Practice in the United States: A Historical Analysis.* Seattle: University of Washington Press, 1983.

Black's Law Dictionary. 6th ed. St. Paul, MN: West Publishing Co., 1990.

Boccaccio, Mary, ed. *Constitutional Issues and Archives: A Collection of Essays from the Fall 1987 Meeting of the Mid-Atlantic Regional Archives Conference, "Archives: The Living Constitution."* N.p.: Mid-Atlantic Regional Archives Conference, 1988.

Boisard, P. "Disposal Policy: Reflections on the Practice of the Archives of the Seine." In *Modern Archives Administration and Records Management: A RAMP Reader*, pp. 209-40. Edited by Peter Walne. Paris: UNESCO, General Information Programme and UNISIST, 1985.

British Columbia. B. C. Archives and Records Service. *Administrative Records Classification System.* Victoria, 1993.

British Columbia Civil Liberties Association. "Right to Public Information and the Protection of Individual Privacy." Vancouver, 1985.

Brown, Robert Craig. "Government and Historian: A Perspective on Bill C43." *Archivaria* 13 (Winter 1981-82): 119-23.

Brubaker, Robert L. "Archival Principles and the Curator of Manuscripts." *American Archivist* 29 (October 1966): 505-14.

Bryans, Victoria. "Towards an Integrated Approach to Public Records Legislation." Paper presented at the Fifth Canadian Records Management Conference, sponsored by ARMA and entitled "Black Gold '89: Capping the Information Explosion." Edmonton, Alberta. February 27 to March 2, 1989.

Buchanan, Scott. "The Public Thing (Res Publica)." In his *So Reason Can Rule: Reflections on Law and Politics*, pp. 105-84. Edited by Stephen Benedict et al. New York: Farrar, Straus and Giroux, 1982.

Buck, Solon J. "Let's Look at the Record." *American Archivist* 8 (April 1945): 109-14.

Bureau of Canadian Archivists. *Toward Descriptive Standards: Report and Recommendations of the Canadian Working Group on Archival Descriptive Standards.* Ottawa: Bureau of Canadian Archivists, 1985.

_____. Planning Committee on Descriptive Standards. *Rules for Archival Description.* Ottawa: Bureau of Canadian Archivists, 1990.

_____. *Subject Indexing for Archives: Report of the Subject Indexing Working Group.* Ottawa: Bureau of Canadian Archivists, 1992.

Burke, E. E. "Some Archival Legislation of the British Commonwealth." *American Archivist* 22 (July 1959): 275-6.

Burke, Frank G. "The Future Course of Archival Theory in the United States." *American Archivist* 44 (Winter 1981): 40-46.

_____. "In Defense of Archival Theory, or Pinkett's Last Charge!" Paper presented at the 52nd Annual General Meeting of the Society of American Archivists. Atlanta, Georgia. September 30, 1988.

Canada. *Access to Information Act. Revised Statutes of Canada.* 1985. Ch. A-1.

_____. *Immigration Act. Revised Statutes of Canada.* 1985. Ch. 1-2.

_____. *National Archives of Canada Act. Revised Statutes of Canada.* 1985. 3rd Supp., 1987. Ch. 1.

Canadian Council of Archives. *The Canadian Archival System: A Report on the National Needs and Priorities of Archives.* Ottawa: Canadian Council of Archives, May 1989.

Cantwell, John. "The 1838 Public Record Office Act and Its Aftermath: A New Perspective." *Journal of the Society of Archivists* 7 (April 1984): 277-86.

_____. *The Public Record Office, 1838-1958.* London: HMSO, 1991.

Cappon, Lester J. "Historical Manuscripts as Archives: Some Definitions and Their Applications." *American Archivist* 19 (April 1956): 101-10.

_____. "What, Then, Is There to Theorize About?" *American Archivist* 45 (Winter 1982): 19-25.

Cencetti, Giorgio. "Il fondamento teorico della dottrina archivistica." *Archivi* VI (1939): 7-13. Reprinted in his *Scritti Archivistici*, pp. 38-46. Roma: Il Centro di Ricerca Editore, 1970.

Chatfield, Helen L. "The Problem of Records From the Standpoint of Management." *American Archivist* 3 (April 1940): 93-101.

Cheney, C. R. "The Records of Medieval England." In his *Medieval Texts and Studies*, pp. 1-15. Oxford: Clarendon Press, 1973.

Chrimes, S. B. *An Introduction to the Administrative History of Medieval England*. 3rd ed. Oxford: Blackwell, 1966.

Clanchy, M. T. *From Memory to Written Record: England 1066-1307*. 2nd ed. Oxford: Blackwell, 1993.

_____. "Remembering the Past and the Good Old Law." *History* 55 (1970): 165-76.

_____. "'Tenacious Letters': Archives and Memory in the Middle Ages." *Archivaria* 11 (Winter 1980-81): 115-25.

Cohen, Morris R., *The Meaning of Human History*. Lasalle, IL: Open Court, The Paul Carus Lectures Series 6, 1947.

_____. *A Preface to Logic*. Cleveland and New York: World Publishing Company, Meridian Books, 1956.

_____. *Reason and Nature: The Meaning of Scientific Method*. 2nd ed. New York: Macmillan, Free Press of Glencoe, 1964.

Cohen, Morris R., and Nagel, Ernest. *An Introduction to Logic and Scientific Method*. New York: Harcourt, Brace & Co., 1934.

Cook, J. Frank. "'Private Papers' of Public Officials." *American Archivist* 38 (July 1975): 299-324.

Cook, Michael. *Archives Administration: A Manual for Intermediate and Smaller Organizations and for Local Government*. Folkestone, England: Dawson, 1977.

_____. *The Management of Information From Archives*. Aldershot, England: Gower Publishing Company, 1986.

Cook, Michael, and Procter, Margaret. *A Manual of Archival Description*. 2nd ed. Aldershot, England: Gower Publishing Company, 1989.

Cook, Terry "ACA Conference Overview." *ACA Bulletin* 12 (July 1988): [1-4].

Cook, Terry, and Wright, Glen T. *General Guide Series 1983: Federal Archives Division*. Ottawa: Public Archives of Canada, 1983.

Corry, J. A., and Hodgetts, J. E. *Democratic Government and Politics*. 3rd edition revised. Toronto: University of Toronto Press, 1959.

Cox, Richard J., and Samuels, Helen W. "The Archivist's First Responsibility: A Research Agenda to Improve the Identification and Retention of Records of Enduring Value," *American Archivist* 51 (Winter and Spring 1988): 28-42.

Crane, Robert Treat. *The State in Constitutional and International Law*. Baltimore, MD: Johns Hopkins Press, 1907.

Daniels, Maygene F. "Introduction to Archival Terminology." In *A Modern Archives Reader: Basic Readings on Archival Theory and Practice*, pp. 336-42. Edited by

Maygene F. Daniels and Timothy Walch. Washington, DC: National Archives and Records Service, 1984.

_____. "Records Appraisal and Disposition." In *Managing Archives and Archival Institutions*, pp. 53-66. Edited by James Gregory Bradsher. Chicago: University of Chicago Press, 1989.

Daniels, Maygene F., and Walch, Timothy, eds. *A Modern Archives Reader: Basic Readings on Archival Theory and Practice.* Washington, DC: National Archives and Records Service, 1984.

Dixon, John. "Freedom of Speech as a Fundamental Right." Position paper adopted by the Board of Directors of the British Columbia Civil Liberties Association. March 13, 1989.

_____. Letter to Trevor Livelton. August 20, 1989. In the possession of the author.

Dollar, Charles M. *Archival Theory and Information Technologies: The Impact of Information Technologies on Archival Principles and Methods.* Macerata, Italy: University of Macerata, Informatics and Documentation Series 1, 1992.

Douglas, David C., and Greenaway, George W., eds. *English Historical Documents, 1042-1189.* London: Eyre & Spottiswoode, 1968.

Dowler, Lawrence. "The Role of Use in Defining Archival Practice and Principles: A Research Agenda for the Availability and Use of Records." *American Archivist* 51 (Winter and Spring 1988): 74-86.

Duchein, Michel. "The Principle of Provenance in Archives Administration." In *Modern Archives Administration and Records Management: A RAMP Reader*, pp. 85-110. Edited by Peter Walne. Paris: UNESCO, General Information Programme and UNISIST, 1985.

Duranti, Luciana. "Comments on Hugh Taylor's and Tom Nesmith's Papers." Paper presented at the 13th Annual Conference of the Association of Canadian Archivists. Windsor, Ontario. June 8, 1988.

_____. "Diplomatics: New Uses for an Old Science." *Archivaria* 28 (Summer 1989): 7-27.

_____. "Diplomatics: New Uses for an Old Science (Part II)." *Archivaria* 29 (Winter 1989-90): 4-17.

_____. "Diplomatics: New Uses for an Old Science (Part III)." *Archivaria* 30 (Summer 1990): 4-20.

_____. "The Odyssey of Records Managers." In two parts. *Records Management Quarterly* 23 (July 1989): 3-11; and *Records Management Quarterly* 23 (October 1989): 3-11.

_____. "Origin and Development of the Concept of Archival Description." *Archivaria* 35 (Spring 1993): 47-54.

Eastwood, Terry. "The Disposition of Ministerial Papers." *Archivaria* 4 (Summer 1977): 3-19.

_____. "Going Nowhere in Particular: The Association of Canadian Archivists Ten Years After." *Archivaria* 21 (Winter 1985-86): 186-90.

_____. Letter to Trevor Livelton. March 21, 1991. In the possession of the author.

_____. "Misunderstandings of Graduate Archival Education." Speech delivered to a session of the Archives Course at the National Archives of Canada. Ottawa, Ontario. October 7, 1987.

_____. "Nailing a Little Jelly to the Wall of Archival Studies." *Archivaria* 35 (Spring 1993): 232-52.

_____. "Nurturing Archival Education in the University." *American Archivist* 51 (Summer 1988): 228-51.

_____. "Nurturing Archival Studies in a Canadian University: A Personal View." Article prepared for publication in the Fall 1988 issue of the *American Archivist*. June 1988.

_____. "Reflections on the Development of Archives in Canada and Australia." In *Archival Documents: Providing Accountability Through Recordkeeping*, pp. 27-39. Edited by Sue McKemmish and Frank Upward. Melbourne: Ancora Press, 1993.

_____. Review of *A Glossary for Archivists, Manuscript Curators, and Records Managers*, by Lewis J. Bellardo and Lynn Lady Bellardo. *American Archivist* 55 (Summer 1992): 493-96.

_____. "Towards a Social Theory of Appraisal." In *The Archival Imagination: Essays in Honour of Hugh A. Taylor*, pp. 71-89. Edited by Barbara L. Craig. Ottawa: Association of Canadian Archivists, 1992.

_____. "Unity and Diversity in the Development of Archival Science in North America." Speech delivered on the occasion of the 25th anniversary of the Special School for Archivists and Librarians at the University of Rome. September 1989.

_____, ed. *The Archival Fonds: From Theory to Practice*. Ottawa: Bureau of Canadian Archivists, Planning Committee on Descriptive Standards, 1992.

Eisenstadt, S. N. *The Political Systems of Empires*. New York: The Free Press of Glencoe, 1963.

Elton, G. R. *England, 1200-1640*. Ithaca, NY: Cornell University Press, The Sources of History, 1969.

Evans, Frank B. "Modern Concepts of Archives Administration and Records Management." *UNESCO Bulletin for Libraries* 24 (1970): 242-47.

Evans, Frank B.; Harrison, Donald F.; and Thompson, Edwin A., comps. "A Basic Glossary for Archivists, Manuscript Curators, and Records Managers." *American Archivist* 37 (July 1974): 415-33.

Evans, Max J. "Authority Control: An Alternative to the Record Group Concept." *American Archivist* 49 (Summer 1986): 249-61.

Felber, Helmut. *Terminology Manual*. Paris: UNESCO, General Information Programme and UNISIST/Infoterm, 1984.

Follett, Wilson. *Modern American Usage: A Guide*. Edited by Jacques Barzun. New York: Hill & Wang, 1966.

Fournier, Frances. "Faculty Papers: Appraisal For Acquisition and Selection." Master of Archival Studies thesis, University of British Columbia, 1990.

Fowler, G. Herbert. *The Care of County Muniments*. Westminster, England: County Councils Association, 1923.

Fox, Christopher John. *Information and Misinformation: An Investigation of the Notions of Information, Misinformation, Informing, and Misinforming*. Westport, CT: Greenwood Press, Contributions in Librarianship and Information Science No. 45, 1983.

Funk & Wagnalls Standard College Dictionary. 1974 Canadian ed.

Galbraith, V. H. *An Introduction to the Use of the Public Records*. Oxford: Clarendon Press, 1934.

_____. *Studies in the Public Records*. London: Thomas Nelson and Sons, 1948.

Gall, Gerald. *The Canadian Legal System*. 2nd ed. Toronto: Carswell Legal Publications, Carswell Student Edition, 1983.

Gracy, David B. *An Introduction to Archives and Manuscripts*. New York: Special Libraries Association, 1981.

_____. "Archivists, You Are What People Think You Keep." *American Archivist* 52 (Winter 1989): 72-78.

Gracy, David B. et al. *Inventories and Registers: A Handbook of Techniques and Examples*. Chicago: Society of American Archivists, 1976.

Graham, Ivor M. Letter to the Editor. *Archives* 7 (October 1966): 237.

Graves, Edgar B., ed. *A Bibliography of English History to 1485*. Oxford: Clarendon Press, 1975.

Great Britain. Parliament. *Modern Public Records, Selection and Access: Report of a Committee Appointed by the Lord Chancellor*. Cmnd. 8204. March 1981.

_____. Parliament. *Report of the Committee on Departmental Records*. Cmnd. 9163. July 1954.

_____. Public Record Office. *First Report of the Deputy Keeper of the Public Records*. London, 1840.

Hall, Hubert. *Studies in English Official Historical Documents*. 1908; rpt. New York: Burt Franklin, 1968.

Hall, Hubert, ed. *Repertory of British Archives*. Vol. 1: *England*. London: Royal Historical Society, 1920.

Ham, F. Gerald. "Public Ownership of the Papers of Public Officials." *American Archivist* 37 (April 1974): 357-58.

Haworth, Kent. "The Principles Speak for Themselves: Articulating a Language of Purpose for Archives." In *The Archival Imagination: Essays in Honour of Hugh A. Taylor*, pp. 90-104. Edited by Barbara L. Craig. Ottawa: Association of Canadian Archivists, 1992.

Hayward, Robert J. "Federal Access and Privacy Legislation and the Public Archives of Canada." *Archivaria* 18 (Summer 1984): 47-57.

Hensen, Steven L. *Archives, Personal Papers, and Manuscripts: A Cataloging Manual for Archival Repositories, Historical Societies, and Manuscript Libraries*. 2nd ed. Chicago: Society of American Archivists, 1989.

Hill, Roscoe R. "Archival Terminology." *American Archivist* 6 (October 1943): 206-11.

_____. "Suggestions on Archival Terminology." *Illinois Libraries* 21 (September 1939): 19.

Hinsley, F. H. *Sovereignty*. London: C.A. Watts & Co., 1966.

Hobbes, Thomas. *Leviathan: Parts I and II*. Edited by Herbert W. Schneider. Indianapolis, IN: Bobbs-Merrill, Library of Liberal Arts, 1958.

Hodnefield, Jacob. "Archives—What Are They?" *American Archivist* 7 (April 1944): 128-29.

Holdsworth, William. *A History of English Law*. 3rd ed. 16 vols. London: Methuen, 1944.

Holmes, Oliver W. "History and Theory of Archival Practice." In *University Archives*, pp. 1-21. Edited by Rolland E. Stevens. Champaigne, IL: University of Illinois, 1965.

_____. "'Public Records'—Who Knows What They Are?" *American Archivist* 23 (January 1960): 3-26.

_____. "Remarks of Oliver W. Holmes." *American Archivist* 25 (April 1962): 238.

Jenkinson, Hilary. *A Manual of Archive Administration*. 2nd ed. 1937; reissued, with an introduction and bibliography by Roger H. Ellis, London: Percy Lund, Humphries & Co., 1965.

_____. "The Classification and Survey of English Archives." In his *Selected Writings of Sir Hilary Jenkinson*, pp. 196-207. Edited by Roger H. Ellis and Peter Walne. Gloucester: Alan Sutton, 1980.

_____. "The English Archivist: A New Profession." In his *Selected Writings of Sir Hilary Jenkinson*, pp. 236-59. Edited by Roger H. Ellis and Peter Walne. Gloucester: Alan Sutton, 1980.

_____. "General Report of a Committee on the Classification of English Archives." In his *Selected Writings of Sir Hilary Jenkinson*, pp. 122-46. Edited by Roger H. Ellis and Peter Walne. Gloucester: Alan Sutton, 1980.

_____. "Modern Archives. Some Reflections on T. R. Schellenberg: *Modern Archives: Principles and Techniques*." *Journal of the Society of Archivists* 1 (April 1957): 147-49.

_____. "Modern Archives. Some Reflections on T. R. Schellenberg: *Modern Archives: Principles and Techniques*." In his *Selected Writings of Sir Hilary Jenkinson*, pp. 339-42. Edited by Roger H. Ellis and Peter Walne. Gloucester: Alan Sutton, 1980.

Johnson, Charles. *The Public Record Office*. London: Society For Promoting Christian Knowledge, Helps for Students of History No. 4, 1918.

Johnson, Samuel. *A Dictionary of the English Language....* London: W. Strathams, 1755.

Jones, Barry. "The Extension of Citizens' Information and Privacy Rights to all Public Bodies in British Columbia: Report Presented to the Honorable Colin Gabelmann, Attorney General and Chair, Cabinet Caucus Committee on Information and Privacy." Victoria: February 1, 1993.

Jones, H. G. *Local Government Records: An Introduction to Their Management, Preservation, and Use*. Nashville, TN: American Association for State and Local History, 1980.

_____. "Presidential Libraries: Is There a Case for a National Presidential Library?" *American Archivist* 38 (July 1975): 325-28.

_____. *The Records of a Nation: Their Management, Preservation, and Use*. New York: Atheneum, 1969.

Jouvenal, Bertrand de. *Sovereignty: An Inquiry Into the Political Good*. Cambridge: Cambridge University Press, 1957.

Kant, Immanuel. *On the Old Saw: That May Be Right in Theory But It Won't Work in Practice*. Translated by G. B. Ashton. Philadelphia: University of Pennsylvania Press, 1974.

Kecskeméti, Charles. "The Professional Culture of the Archivist." *American Archivist* 50 (Summer 1987): 408-13.

Kimball, Gregg D. "The Burke-Cappon Debate: Some Further Criticisms and Considerations for Archival Theory." *American Archivist* 48 (Fall 1985): 369-76.

Knightbridge, A. A. H. "National Archives Policy." *Journal of the Society of Archivists* 7 (October 1983): 213-23.

Lamb, W. Kaye. "The Changing Role of the Archivist." *American Archivist* 29 (January 1966): 3-10.

"The Last Dramatic Questions." *MANAS* 29 (31 March 1976): 1-8.

Leavitt, Arthur H. "What Are Archives?" *American Archivist* 24 (April 1961): 175-78.

Lemieux, Victoria. "Archival Solitudes: The Impact on Appraisal and Acquisition of Legislative Concepts of Records and Archives." *Archivaria* 35 (Spring 1993): 153-61.

Lewis, C. S. *The Discarded Image: An Introduction to Medieval and Renaissance Literature.* Cambridge: Cambridge University Press, 1964.

_____. *Studies in Words.* Cambridge: Cambridge University Press, 1960.

Livelton, Trevor. "Some Thoughts on the Archival Function and Method, With a Note on Their Relation to the Arsenal of the Forum." Term paper for ARST 500, School of Library, Archival and Information Studies, University of British Columbia. September 1988.

Lodolini, Elio. "The War of Independence of Archivists." *Archivaria* 28 (Summer 1989): 36-47.

López, Pedro. "Archival Training: Specialists and/or Generalists." Paper prepared for the XIIth International Congress on Archives. Montreal. September 1992.

Love, J. H. "What are Records?" *Archives and Manuscripts* 14 (May 1986): 54-60.

Lyon, Bryce. *A Constitutional and Legal History of Medieval England.* 2nd ed. New York: W. W. Norton, 1980.

Machlup, Fritz. "Semantic Quirks in Studies of Information." In *The Study of Information: Interdisciplinary Messages*, pp. 641-71. Edited by Fritz Machlup and Una Mansfield. New York: John Wiley & Sons, 1983.

Mackinnon, Charles, and Czerny, Robert. "Managing the Records of a Minister's Office." *The Archivist* 16 (September-October 1989): 2-4.

Maclean, Ian. "Australian Experience in Record and Archives Management." *American Archivist* 22 (October 1959): 387-418.

MacNeil, Heather. *Without Consent: The Ethics of Disclosing Personal Information in Public Archives.* Metuchen, NJ: Society of American Archivists and Scarecrow Press, 1992.

"The Making of Hypotheses." *MANAS* 2 (27 July 1949): 6-7.

Matters, Marion, ed. *Automated Records and Techniques in Archives: A Resource Directory.* Chicago: Society of American Archivists, 1990.

Meiklejohn, Alexander. *Alexander Meiklejohn, Teacher of Freedom: A Collection of His Writings and a Biographical Study.* Edited by Cynthia Stokes Brown. Berkeley, CA: Meiklejohn Civil Liberties Institute, Studies in Law and Social Change No. 2, 1981.

_____. *Education Between Two Worlds.* 1942; rpt. New York: Atherton, Atheling Books, 1965.

_____. *Political Freedom: The Constitutional Powers of the People.* 1960; rpt. Westport, CT: Greenwood Press, 1979.

_____. *What Does America Mean?* 1935; rpt. New York: W. W. Norton & Company, The Norton Library, 1972.

Merriam, C. E., Jr. *History of the Theory of Sovereignty Since Rousseau.* 1900; rpt. New York: AMS Press, 1968.

Mitchell, Gary. "Do Archives Have A Future?" Paper presented at the 12th Annual Meeting of the Association of Canadian Archivists. Hamilton, Ontario. June 6, 1987.

Morddel, Anne. "The Delusion of Accountability." *Records Management Quarterly* 24 (July 1990): 42, 44-45.

Muller S., Feith J. A., and Fruin, R. *Manual for the Arrangement and Description of Archives.* 2nd ed. Translated by Arthur H. Leavitt. 1940; reissued, with a new foreword by Ken Munden, New York: H. W. Wilson, 1968.

Mullet, Charles F. "The 'Better Reception, Preservation, and More Convenient Use' of Public Records in Eighteenth-Century England." *American Archivist* 27 (April 1964): 195-217.

Mykland, Liv. "Protection and Integrity: The Archivist's Identity and Professionalism." Paper prepared for the XIIth International Congress on Archives. Montreal. September 1992.

Natason, Maurice, ed. *Philosophy of the Social Sciences.* New York: Random House, 1963.

National Archives and Records Administration. *Personal Papers of Executive Branch Officials: A Management Guide.* Washington, DC: National Archives and Records Administration, Management Guide Series, 1992.

_____. *Select List of Publications of the National Archives and Records Administration.* Washington, DC: National Archives and Records Administration, General Information Leaflet No. 3, 1986.

National Archives of Canada. Program Evaluation and Research Policy Branch. *Acquisition Evaluation Study.* Vol. 2: *Research Reports.* November 1987.

Nelson, Anna Kasten, ed. *The Records of Federal Officials: A Selection of Materials from the National Study Commission on Records and Documents of Federal Officials.* New York: Garland Publishing, 1978.

Newsome, A. R. "The Proposed Uniform State Public Records Act." *American Archivist* 3 (April 1940): 107-15.

Nock, Albert Jay. "Imposter Terms." In his *Free Speech and Plain Language,* pp. 285-304. 1937; rpt. Freeport, NY: Books For Libraries Press, 1968.

Nokes, G. D. *An Introduction to Evidence.* 4th ed. London: Sweet & Maxwell, 1967.

Norton, Margaret Cross. *Norton on Archives: The Writings of Margaret Cross Norton on Archival & Records Management.* Edited by Thornton W. Mitchell. Carbondale: Southern Illinois University Press, 1975.

O'Toole, James M. "On the Idea of Permanence." *American Archivist* 52 (Winter 1989): 10-25.

Otten, Klaus W. "Basis for a Science of Information." In *Information Science: Search for Identity,* pp. 91-106. Edited by Anthony Debons. New York: Marcel Dekker, 1974.

Owen, A. E. B. "The Terminology of Archives: A Review." *Archives* 7 (April 1965): 57-58.

Oxford English Dictionary. 2nd ed. 20 vols. Oxford: Clarendon Press, 1989.

Palm, Charles G. "Introduction to Archival Research Agendas." *American Archivist* 51 (Winter and Spring 1988): 24-27.

Parkinson, Jane. "Accountability in Archival Science." Master of Archival Studies thesis, University of British Columbia, 1993.

Partridge, Eric. *Origins: A Short Etymological Dictionary of Modern English.* 2nd ed. New York: Macmillan, 1959.

Pederson, Ann E. "Writing and Research." Paper prepared for the XIIth International Congress on Archives. Montreal. September 1992.

Peterson, Gary M., and Peterson, Trudy Huskamp. *Archives and Manuscripts: Law.* Chicago: Society of American Archivists, Basic Manual Series, 1985.

Plato. *Meno.* Translated by W. K. C. Guthrie. In *Plato: The Collected Dialogues,* pp. 353-84. Edited by Edith Hamilton and Huntington Cairns. Princeton, NJ: Princeton University Press, Bollingen Series 71, 1961.

_____. *The Republic of Plato.* Translated with an introduction and notes by Francis MacDonald Cornford. London: Oxford University Press, 1941.

Pollock, Frederick, and Maitland, Frederic William. *TheHistory of English Law Before the Time of Edward I.* 2nd ed. 2 vols. 1898; reissued, with a new introduction and select bibliography by S. F. C. Milsom. Cambridge: Cambridge University Press, 1968.

Posner, Ernst. *Archives in the Ancient World.* Cambridge, MA: Harvard University Press, 1972.

_____. "The National Archives and the Archival Theorist." In his *Archives and the Public Interest: Selected Essays by Ernst Posner,* pp. 131-40. Edited by Ken Munden. Washington, DC: Public Affairs Press, 1967.

Pugh, D. S., ed. *Organization Theory: Selected Readings.* 2nd ed. Harmondsworth, England: Penguin Books, 1984.

Radoff, Morris. "What Should Bind Us Together." *AmericanArchivist* 19 (January 1956): 3-9.

Raffel, Stanley. *Matters of Fact: A Sociological Inquiry.* London: Routledge & Kegan Paul, 1979.

Rapport, Leonard. "No Grandfather Clause: Reappraising Accessioned Records." In *A Modern Archives Reader: Basic Readings on Archival Theory and Practice,* pp. 80-90. Edited by Maygene F. Daniels and Timothy Walch. Washington, DC: National Archives and Records Service, 1984.

Reese, W.L. *Dictionary of Philosophy and Religion: Eastern and Western Thought.* Atlantic Highlands, NJ: Humanities Press, 1980.

Richardson, G.D. Letter to the Editor. *Archives* 7 (April 1966): 166.

Robek, Mary F.; Brown, Gerald F.; and Maedke, Wilmer O. *Information and Records Management.* 3rd ed. Encino, CA: Glencoe Publishing Company, 1987.

Roberts, John W. "Archival Theory: Much Ado About Shelving." *American Archivist* 50 (Winter 1987): 66-74.

_____. "Archival Theory: Myth or Banality?" *American Archivist* 53 (Winter 1990): 110-20.

Robinson, Richard. *Definition.* Oxford: The Clarendon Press, 1968.

Rodgers, Daniel T. *Contested Truths: Keywords in American Politics Since Independence.* New York: Basic Books, 1987.

Roszak, Theodore. *The Cult of Information: The Folklore of Computers and the True Art of Thinking.* New York: Pantheon, 1986.

Rousseau, Jean Jacques. *The Social Contract.* An eighteenth-century translation revised and edited by Charles Frankel. New York: Hafner Press, 1947.

Rushton, Herbert J. "Opinion From the Office of the Attorney General." *American Archivist* 6 (January 1943): 70-71.

Samuels, Helen. "Who Controls the Past." *American Archivist* 49 (Spring 1986): 109-24.

Schaar, John H. "Legitimacy in the Modern State." In his *Legitimacy in the Modern State,* pp. 15-51. New Brunswick, NJ: Transaction Books, 1981.

Schellenberg, T. R. *The Appraisal of Modern Public Records.* Washington, DC: National Archives of the United States, Bulletin No. 8, 1956.

_____. *The Management of Archives.* New York: Columbia University Press, 1965.

_____. *Modern Archives: Principles and Techniques.* Chicago: University of Chicago Press, 1956.

_____. "Principles of Archival Appraisal." In *Modern Archives Administration and Records Management: A RAMP Reader,* pp. 269-79. Edited by Peter Walne. Paris: UNESCO, General Information Programme and UNISIST, 1985.

Schleisinger, Arthur, Jr. "Foreword." In *The Records of Federal Officials: A Selection of Materials from the National Study Commission on Records and Documents of Federal Officials,* pp. ix-xiv. Edited by Anna Kasten Nelson. New York: Garland Publishing, 1978.

Schrader, Alvin M. "Toward A Theory of Library and Information Science." Diss. Indiana 1983.

Scott, Robert W. "Governor's Records: Public Records." *American Archivist* 33 (January 1970): 5-10.

Seeskin, Kenneth R. "Never Speculate, Never Explain: The State of Contemporary Philosophy." *American Scholar* 49 (Winter 1979-80): 19-33.

Seton, Rosemary E. *The Preservation and Administration of Private Archives: A RAMP Study.* Paris: UNESCO, General Information Programme and UNISIST, 1984.

Sheppard, A. F. "Records and Archives in Court." *Archivaria* 19 (Winter 1984-85): 196-203.

Shipley, Joseph T. *Dictionary of Word Origins.* 1945; rpt. Totowa, NJ: Littlefield, Adams & Co., 1967.

Smith, Clive. "Glossary of Terminology." In *Keeping Archives,* pp. 355-65. Edited by Ann Pederson. Sydney: Australian Society of Archivists, 1987.

Society of American Archivists. Committee on Education and Professional Development. *Guidelines for the Development of a Curriculum for a Master of Archival Studies: Draft.* Chicago: Society of American Archivists, 1993.

Somerville, Robert. "Archives or Records?" *Archives* 7 (October 1965): 193-94.

Stephenson, Mary Sue. "Deciding Not to Build the Wall: Research and the Archival Profession." *Archivaria* 32 (Summer 1991): 145-51.

Stielow, Frederick J. "Archival Theory Redux and Redeemed: Definition and Context Toward a General Theory." *American Archivist* 54 (Winter 1991): 14-26.

Stuart-Stubbs, Basil. "Keynote Address: Whither Information?" In *Management of Recorded Information: Converging Disciplines; Proceedings of the International Council on Archives' Symposium on Current Records; National Archives of Canada, Ottawa, May 15-17, 1989,* pp. 15-26. Compiled by Cynthia J. Durance. Munich: K. G. Saur, 1990.

Taylor, Hugh. "'My Very Act and Deed': Some Reflections on The Role of Textual Records in the Conduct of Affairs." *American Archivist* 51 (Fall 1988): 456-69.

Thomas, F. S. *Notes of Materials for the History of Public Departments.* London, 1846.

Tussman, Joseph. *The Burden of Office: Agamemnon and Other Losers.* Vancouver: Talonbooks, 1989.

_____. *Experiment at Berkeley.* London: Oxford University Press, 1969.

_____. *Government and the Mind.* New York: Oxford University Press, 1977.

_____. *Obligation and the Body Politic.* London: Oxford University Press, 1960.

Ullmann, Walter. *Law and Politics in the Middle Ages: An Introduction to the Sources of Medieval Political Ideas.* Ithaca, NY: Cornell University Press, The Sources of History, 1975.

United States. *Freedom of Information Act.* 5 *United States Code.* Sec. 552.

_____. National Archives. *Third Annual Report of the Archivist of the United States For the Fiscal Year Ending 30 June 1937.* Washington, DC, 1938.

Vaughan, Joseph F., ed. "Senate Debate on Public Records." *American Archivist* 10 (July 1947): 258-62.

Walne, Peter. Letter to the Editor. *Archives* 7 (April 1966): 163-66.

_____. "The Record Commissions, 1800-37." In *Prisca Munimenta: Studies in Archival & Administrative History Presented to Dr* [sic] *A.E.J. Hollaender,* pp. 9-18. Edited by Felicity Ranger. London: University of London Press, 1973.

_____, ed. *Dictionary of Archival Terminology.* Munich: K. G. Saur, 1984.

Weber, Max. *Economy and Society: An Outline of Interpretive Sociology.* 3 vols. Translated by Ephraim Fischoff et al. Edited by Guenther Roth and Claus Wittich. New York: Bedminster Press, 1968.

_____. *The Theory of Social and Economic Organization.* Translated by A. M. Henderson and Talcott Parsons. Edited by Talcott Parsons. New York: The Free Press, 1964.

Weilbrenner, Bernard. "L'homme politique et ses archives: papiers publics ou privés?" *Archives* 10 (Décembre 1978): 35-41.

Weizenbaum, Joseph. *Computer Power and Human Reason: From Judgment to Calculation.* 1976; rpt., with a new preface, Harmondsworth, England: Penguin, 1984.

Williams, Raymond. *Keywords: A Vocabulary of Culture and Society.* London: Fontana/Croom Helm, 1976.

Wilsted, Thomas and Nolte, William. *Managing Archival and Manuscript Repositories.* Chicago: Society of American Archivists, Archival Fundamentals Series, 1991.

Wolff, Robert Paul. *In Defense of Anarchism.* New York: Harper and Row, Harper Colophon Books, 1976.

Wood, David N. "Management of Grey Literature." In *Management of Recorded Information: Converging Disciplines; Proceedings of the International Council on Archives' Symposium on Current Records; National Archives of Canada, Ottawa, May 15-17 1989,* pp. 61-68. Compiled by Cynthia J. Durance. Munich: K. G. Saur, 1990.

Index

About the Author

Trevor Livelton (B.A., M.A.S., Brit. Col.) has worked with public and private records in a variety of settings. A graduate of the Master of Archival Studies program at the University of British Columbia, he is presently an archivist with the City of Victoria.